FAST-TRACK
CAREERS

A Gu~~ide to the Best J~~obs

New

Publisher: Stephen Kippur
Editor: Katherine S. Bolster
Managing Editor: Andrew B. Hoffer
Editing, Design & Production: Publications Development Co.

This publication is designed to provide accurate and authoritative information in regard to the subject matter covered. It is sold with the understanding that the publisher is not engaged in rendering legal, accounting, or other professional service. If legal advice or other expert assistance is required, the services of a competent professional person should be sought. *From a declaration of principles jointly adopted by a committee of The American Bar Association and a committee of publishers.*

Library of Congress Cataloging-in-Publication Data

Lewis, William, 1946–
  Fast-track careers.

  1. Vocational guidance—United States.   2. Success
in business—United States.   3. Executives—Employment—
United States.   4. Baby boom generation—United States.
I. Schuman, Nancy.   II. Title.
HF5382.5.U5L45   1987   331.7′02′0973   87-10045
ISBN 0-471-83801-2   (paper)
ISBN 0-471-63564-2   (cloth)

Printed in the United States of America
  10 9 8 7 6 5 4 3 2

ACKNOWLEDGMENTS

The authors would like to thank the following people for their valuable and generous contributions to this book:

- Katherine Schowalter Bolster, our editor at John Wiley, for her unfailing support and patience.
- L. A. Davidson, William Grey Maliawco, Paula Harvey, Judith Levy, and Donna Chisholm for their research and interviews.
- Ghenia Websterss, who coordinated the production of this manuscript.
- And special thanks and praise to Nancy Molloy, our research and writing assistant, for her tireless energy and commitment to this project—her efforts made the book a reality.

WILLIAM LEWIS
NANCY SCHUMAN

OTHER CAREERS BOOKS FROM WILEY

CONTENTS

INTRODUCTION

Some people pay their dues and some people are "doers." What the doers, a rather small group, are doing is making it big and making it young. We call them "Fast-Trackers"— they're the under-40 set who have managed to step in one swift motion from the classroom to the corner office with a view. Many have incomes double or triple their ages. How nice to be 28 and bringing home a paycheck in excess of $100,000 a year!

In this book, we've focused on eight fast-track career areas where a doer—an achiever—can go for both the money and the glory without rich parents or many years of school preparing for careers in medicine or law. By no means, however, should you limit your aspirations to the industries or career areas we've noted here. Fast-trackers are found in new endeavors of all kinds. If you are ambitious, clever, and a workaholic, you have what it takes to become a fast-tracker.

Our book is a resource for you which describes some fields where a high school or college graduate—particularly a liberal arts major—can write his or her own success story.

After considerable research, we've selected

- Finance
- Advertising
- Media
- Real estate
- Executive search
- Sales
- Hospitality
- Entrepreneurship

as the fields we will describe because, in our opinion, they offer unique opportunities for fast-tracking.

As placement professionals in New York's leading personnel service, we are constantly meeting young careerists eager to make their fame and fortune quickly. There is a special combination of talent, location, and industry that allows fast-tracking to happen. And because we are often questioned for career advice, we were prompted to write this guide.

It is true that some industries lend themselves to high salaries and an atmosphere of glamor. The areas we have targeted are not the only fields in which an ambitious individual can make a name quickly. In virtually any industry, there will be those people who shine a little bit brighter than the rest.

Within each chapter you'll find a profile of the industry, facts about entry-level opportunities, who the industry giants are, and what the expected earnings are. Also included is a glossary of industry lingo and suggested further reading.

Read on to see if your talents or interests match up with the skills and activities of these fast-tracking fields. We wish you success and a hefty paycheck!

1

WANTING IT ALL

Changing lifestyles and a new emphasis on careers have reshaped our traditional work ethic. Many young careerists want it all—the trappings of success, wealth, prestige, a luxury condo, and a Porsche in the driveway—and they want it all *now*.

This concept of "having it all" has become a big part of young America's career expectations. A positive economy has given birth to an optimistic group of young people who are committed to consumerism. Occasionally labeled the "gimme generation," they are more a generation of affluence than of selfishness. These upwardly mobile baby boomers—people born between 1946 and 1964—personify the phenomenon of fast-tracking.

To qualify as a "fast-tracker" one must hold a managerial or executive position and have an annual income of $50,000 or more by the time one turns thirty. One 27-year-old fast-tracker reflects, "I find that I'm suddenly in a rather enviable position; everyone wants what I have." What she has is a vice presidency, a six-figure income, and a sense of self satisfaction at home and at work.

This ambitious young woman's path to success began while she was still in school. In fact, today's college campuses are crowded with achievement-oriented students preoccupied with their careers. At today's prices, a college education is so expensive that students feel bound to regard it as an investment—and one that must pay off. The graduates are unwilling to wait years for the pay off, they want their return on investment sooner . . . not later.

In direct contrast to the activists of the sixties, who scorned materialism, are the students of the eighties. Now they sport pin-striped suits and are more likely to talk investments than free love. Students have refocused their concerns and while the welfare of the world at large is still an issue, it is now considered okay to expend energy on one's own goals and career/life aspirations.

Whether you love or hate fast-tracking and all that goes with it, no one can deny that a high-paying career has its own rewards. In addition to a healthy income, a fast-track position is usually associated with good times, excitement, and a certain sense of risk. Of course you can't be a fast-tracker without making sacrifices, or at the very least, occasional trade-offs. One success-driven individual admits, "I'm never completely satisfied with where I am, so I push myself a little harder, work a little later, and even forego some personal relationships. What I get in return is a natural high for me. . . . You can't go after a powerful career without knowing you will have extreme highs and lows, and lots of pressure. I happen to love my life, but I would only recommend it to people who have a clear sense of self. You need to keep refocusing your goals and never become smug about your achievements."

NEW CANDIDATES FOR SUCCESS

Big bucks and positions of power are no longer solely the rewards of an MBA degree or an undergraduate business diploma. Employers are now eager for graduates of programs in the humanities and liberal arts who have the necessary credentials. Why? The consensus is that employers have begun to recognize the value of a well-rounded education, particularly when it is combined with a high academic average.

According to Mary Giannini, Executive Director of the Center for Career Services Office at Columbia University, "Business discovered somewhere along the line that liberal arts graduates were extremely valuable and extremely productive; employers then revamped their campus recruitment efforts in response to this awareness."

David S. Bechtel, Director of the Career Development and Placement Center at the University of Illinois Urbana comments, "Clearly, IBM, AT&T, Proctor & Gamble, Prudential, Northern Trust Bank, Quaker Oats, Xerox, and Morgan Guaranty Trust are all hiring liberal arts graduates. The job titles vary widely, but the common thread seems to be that they're looking for entry-level generalists with lots of potential."

Many liberal arts graduates do hedge their bets. Sprinkled throughout their four-year programs are key courses in economics, organizational behavior, and computer science. Such diversified training enables the fast-tracking liberal arts student to enjoy greater mobility within the corporate structure.

Because of the recent MBA-degree holding glut of candidates in the job market, many companies have turned to hiring top-ranking liberal arts graduates who are often under-recruited and extremely qualified. Companies now hire the 22-year-old Bachelor of Arts or Bachelor of Science graduate at a $25,000 a year salary rather than the 24- or 25-year-old MBA holder who commands a salary of $40,000 a year or more. They will train the B.A. or B.S. in the firm's own philosophy and produce an exceptional, experienced manager at the ripe old age of twenty-six. The initial salary outlay is lower, the overall investment of time is the same, so a company may feel that the return on investment is therefore greater.

At the University of Texas, Howard Figler, Director of the Career Development Center, is quick to point out, "Business will always choose the student they think is the brightest. When it comes down to it, serious companies care less about what your grade point average happens to be, or what you studied; they want to get the person they believe has the most potential. If that happens to be a religious studies major who expresses himself or herself extremely well, and who seems to have that certain 'spark'—then that's who they'll hire."

For people just starting out, a generalist position can be the first step to success. They enter a field with the advantage of a wide range of entry-level openings. The smart, aspiring fast-tracker gets a good grounding in bottom-line operations and is soon able to channel that expertise into a few critical areas. After one or two years sharpening this expertise and getting a reputation as the organization's in-house expert in a specific area of the business, greater challenges and responsibilities beckon. The man or woman who is upwardly mobile is ready to take these challenges on and moves back into general management. These people have built careers with roots in both a speciality or technical area of the business and in management and basic operations as well. The process may take anywhere from three to eight years, with an average fast-tracker spending six years to build up a power base.

Into the late 1980s and well into the 1990s, businesses will be faced with fewer and fewer college graduates. In the future, companies will compete for the top graduates, rather than the top graduates competing for companies.

SUCCESS AS AN OBSESSION

For the baby-boom population, the importance of success grew out of the post-1980 economic recession. Although many view the obsession with success as materialism—a pursuit of luxury—some psychologists suggest it is really an attempt to avoid the anxiety that comes from the experience of unemployment and a lack of income or the threat of these conditions. Success represents security, self-esteem, and the means to indulge in the "good life." We have nurtured an affluent generation and many of the under-40 set are simply not content with a promise of success sometime in the future.

"I want it now!" is the battle cry of an aspiring fast-tracker. This is not the howl of a spoiled child throwing a tantrum, but rather the precept of an adult who thrives on energy, hard work, professionalism, and who possesses a healthy appreciation of consumerism and material well-being.

At the outset, we want to emphasize that no one says it will be easy to achieve such success, nor do we say it will come instantly. Success calls for a deep commitment to your career, which often becomes your number one priority. Are you ready for an average work week of 50 to 60 hours or more? Can you cheerfully respond to being labeled a "workaholic," often by friends as well as family? The whole concept requires that you exercise your brain as faithfully as athletes exercise their bodies. It is an exhausting (and exhilarating) lifestyle, but it is clearly not without its own rewards.

WHO MAKES IT?

Teaching someone how to be a fast-tracker is a little like trying to make a righthanded person out of a lefty. If there isn't some innate special ability or talent, it just won't happen. However, people with potential who are stalled in stagnant careers, or graduating seniors on the verge of career choices may find that some informal training can make the big difference.

But who *really* makes it big? We have all known people who were voted the most likely to succeed but who went nowhere. And, we have seen others we thought of as zeros turn into heros! How does it happen? Do the big successes—the heros—have any traits in common? **Yes**, they do, these traits are discussed next.

A Clear Sense of Goals

They know what they want and they go after it. They conceive of the step-by-step route they must follow in terms of rank and title in order to reach their career objectives. At each point in their professional life, they measure their achievements and status against what it is they are aiming for.

Financial Self-Worth

A true fast-tracker knows what he or she wants to be earning. As their careers develop, they set specific financial goals so that they can put a dollar value on their success. If the field they are in doesn't promise the big bucks that they want—they get out. They go where the money is.

Experience or Seasoning

This is true even for recent graduates. Every new work experience is seen as a learning test that builds credentials and expands the overall knowledge of a chosen career area.

A Willingness to Take Risks

No guts, no glory . . . people who play it safe with their careers will never be fast-trackers. This means taking on new challenges and never allowing yourself to be too comfortable. One young dynamo told us, "If I'm not a little bit scared, then it's not worth doing."

An Ability to Spot a Trend and Profit by It

Fast-trackers are always first. Maybe others had the same idea, but the doers are the people who move on it and profit by it. Some are entrepreneurs who stake out their own territories and build their own empires. Others (those who remain part of an organization that they do not own), demonstrate an "intrapreneurial" spirit. Like entrepreneurs, they create new products or services (for their "adopted" companies), are credited with its innovation, and are usually given full control over its development.

Exceptional People Skills

Fast-trackers are team players who have learned how to motivate and manage others. They exhibit excellent listening skills and have discovered the secret of making those people around them feel important, thereby inspiring loyalty from support staff and peers.

Savvy

Essential for survival, it is quick thinking, business smarts, and image all in one package—the ability to function like a real work horse while conveying the impression of a thoroughbred.

TOMORROW'S EXECUTIVES: HOW THEY MAY BE DIFFERENT

Generalizations are difficult to make. But according to management experts, some broad differences do exist between today's executives and tomorrow's. These differences are summarized in Table 1.

Table 1

The *Old* Generation	The *New* Generation*
Cautious	Eager to take risks
Insecure	Optimistic
Resistant to change	Flexible
Loyal to company	Willing to job-hop
Value job security	Want to make impact
Male	Male or female
White	Ethnically diverse
"A good day's work"	Workaholic
Comfortable in bureaucracies	Crave autonomy, power
Conservative Republican	Independent
People-oriented	Numbers-oriented
Slide rules, legal pads	Computers, data networks
College degree	Advanced degrees
25-year career plan	Instant gratification

*Reprinted from November 10, 1986 issue of *Business Week* by special permission, © 1986 by McGraw Hill, Inc.

MAKING IT WORK FOR YOU

Putting yourself in the right place at the right time is only one ingredient to early success. We interviewed dozens of fast-trackers and asked them how they had achieved their commendable status. Many spoke freely "off the record," preferring to keep their strategies for success anonymous. They agreed that the length of time one spends at a specific employer is never a factor. Instead it is *performance* and *power*.

Performance is a singular talent. You must be *more than good* at what you do, you must be a star.

Power however, is built through contact with others and the ability to make relationships work in your favor. Fast-tracking has a great deal to do with office politics and power relationships. You have got to be a tough campaigner who makes a point of getting to know everybody. Perhaps the biggest mistake you, as an ambitious employee can make, is to ignore the office grapevine. It is foolish and naive to dismiss it as idle gossip. In addition to learning who is dating whom, you find out from the grapevine who is rising to the top, who has taken which side of a current controversy and who or what are management's pets as well as their peeves. It is all knowledge and *knowledge is the key to power.*

A word about power: If you are afraid of it, you will not enjoy fast-tracking. Powerholders (clients as well as internal management) are at an organization's core. If you truly aspire to excel in your field, you must penetrate this power nucleus. Once you do, you will acquire your own sense of power. Even those who do not want power for themselves respect it and are influenced by it. You will find that people cooperate more easily with those in authority. Fast-trackers learn to take control of events.

How do you build a power base? Examine the two distinct power systems within your organization. There is the formal flowchart, where every employee's name, title, and position is clearly displayed. Then there is the informal alliance system, which is a much more accurate measure of an organization's operational flow. It is often based on the premise of "I'll help you, if you'll help me." This informal power system may, in fact, wield the real power in the organization. Furthermore, your entrance into the "informal fast-track" may be far more important than your official promotion.

High achievers get along with the clerical support staff and the mailroom personnel as well as the top brass. Ignoring the executive secretary of a vice president or chairperson won't help your ambitions. You never know whose help you will need to get that big project out, and mailroom workers are often in charge of photocopying and overnight packages. If you have stepped on anyone's toes in the past, it will inevitably come back to haunt you.

Here are some guidelines for building a power base of your own.

- Don't be shy. Meet everyone you possibly can.
- Do your homework. Study both the formal and informal power systems that surround you. Cultivate power relationships after determining who it is at your company that *really* makes things happen. You may be surprised to find where the power lies.
- Know who the fast-trackers are in the organization.
- Network through trade associations. Become familiar with well-known professionals who work in your industry, but who are members of the competition's team. Look for friendships among the opposition's ranks.
- Be extremely image conscious. Observe the written (or unwritten) company dress code. Take your most important cues from the boss. Appear as professional as possible.
- Ask for more responsibility. Never wait for projects, accounts, or departments, to come your way. To keep your own enthusiasm and interest high (as well as to grab management's eye), express your need for new challenges. Be assertive and demonstrate initiative.

THE PITFALLS OF FAST-TRACKING

If you are reading our advice and are finding it a little bit frightening and self-centered . . . good for you! It does require one to be aggressive and unrelenting in attaining one's career goals, but it doesn't necessarily mean you should lose sight of who you are or your ability to show compassion and to care for yourself and others.

There is where the danger lies: Push yourself so far that you no longer know who you are or what you are about. A successful career does not in itself guarantee contentment or self satisfaction. Fast-trackers are quick to recognize that they are not always happy. Often they are assailed by a feeling of, "Is that all there is?" and it is puzzling and sometimes debilitating. After all, they have it all, don't they?

It would not be fair to encourage you on the path to riches and power without offering some insight as to how those who have made it feel about their success.

Security vs. Serendipity

You are a product of changing lifestyles and conflicting goals. The passion of the sixties left us a legacy of individuality, a pioneering spirit, and a burning desire to be socially useful. The next decade, the seventies, emphasized the need for security and glorified putting one's own interests first— "Look out for number one." Those years, in turn, laid the groundwork for the eighties, which finds young careerists wanting the best of both worlds.

In our conversations with numerous high achievers, we found an unsettling theme running through success stories in several fields. Said one Wall Street whiz, "I can't help but wonder if I've sold out. Is this what I really want?" Human behavior experts agree that fast-tracking takes an emotional and psychological toll on its participants. Successful careerists are prone to emotional and physical disorders, often complaining of aches and pains in the head, stomach, and back and gastrointestinal problems. They are depressed, have anxiety attacks, a feeling of emptiness, a dislike of self, insomnia, and fatigue.

Consumerist Behavior

Careerists *must* keep a clear perspective on their personal lifestyles and work styles or they may develop a selfish and/or *consumerist* attitude. Most recently this consumerism was associated with the term "yuppie" which implied early success and comfortable living. For some fast-trackers, dealing with the compromises of career success, causes them to turn to buying and acquiring possessions as a means of escape and rationalization. Furthermore, social and personal relationships often suffer. There is a tendency to judge people (friends, lovers, and coworkers) in terms of "What can he or she do for me?" Unfortunately, the fast lane is overflowing with shallow relationships and a never-ending search to find an elusive someone who will meet a fast-tracker's idealistic expectations. Beware of piling up possessions and power in an attempt to fill the void of human contact.

Solutions?

We firmly believe that you *can* get beyond these pitfalls or else we would not have written this book. In pointing out potential dangers we hope we will be able to help you avoid, or at least recognize mistakes you might make. We encourage all careerists or future careerists struggling with the inconsistencies of career advancement and self fulfillment to do the following:

- Work on developing a life outside of the office.
- Get healthy . . . eat right, exercise, rest, and learn to relax.
- Pursue and value family pleasure and friendships.
- Devote time and energy to a voluntary cause where you are *not* paid for your contributions.
- Find an outlet for interests beyond your career—take up a sport, find a hobby, take a walk on the beach . . . indulge yourself in mini pleasures and a sense of freedom from work.

Plateauing

One other danger associated with fast-track fever is "plateauing." When work stops being a source of enjoyment, it is time to re-evaluate what you are doing. Maybe you are bored, or you feel as though you were caught in a vacuum. If that's the case, you are on the fringes of plateauing and you should begin to listen to yourself when you are speaking of your job to others. Does it sound as though you like what you do? Are you finding and meeting new challenges? Is there a degree of enthusiasm when you express yourself?

Plateauing isn't necessarily bad. It simply means you need to get outside yourself and look at your career with objective eyes. The real mistake comes when fast-trackers won't admit to themselves that they are plateauing. If you fail to recognize the symptoms of plateauing, you will soon be on your way to "burn-out." If you are a compulsive over-achiever, you may have difficulty in accepting plateauing as anything except a form of failure. This may be a problem that is perceptual.

Instead of failure, try to think of yourself in terms of being "blocked" or "clogged." Examine the situation; can you modify it or is getting out the only reasonable alternative? If you can and want to save your career, several fast-trackers recommend a lateral transfer. This is an option that often is not considered because it usually means a change of position without increased compensation or an elevation in title or status. It is a good option however, if it means adding new skills to your repertoire, building a larger staff for yourself, or increasing your overall visibility within the company.

IS IT WORTH IT? —————————————————

The young successes we spoke with clearly think so. That is not to say you do not have to work at your career, as well as your personal life. Dream jobs that offer power and wealth are tremendously hard to find and they are never, ever easy to maintain. If you are still eager to pursue the fast-tracking life after reading our list of the problems you are likely to encounter, we applaud you. In not turning back you are already exhibiting that sense of risk which is so exceedingly important.

FAST-TRACKING CITIES

People who want power—people who play hard and work hard—people who are out for success—naturally gravitate toward the cities with the same qualities. We have attempted to note major metropolitan areas where a fast-track lifestyle is both possible and probable. Listed are those cities offering excellent prospects for business throughout this decade and into the 1990s. (*Source:* Savvy, "The Right Place," New York: Savvy Company, November 1985)

Anchorage, Alaska

Austin, Texas

Burlington, Vermont

Chicago, Illinois

Columbus, Ohio

Denver, Colorado

Los Angeles, California

Minneapolis/St. Paul, Minnesota

Nashville, Tennessee

New York, New York

Portland, Maine

San Francisco, California

Stamford, Connecticut

Tampa, Florida

Washington, D.C.

These cities were selected based on the area's population, major industries, number of Fortune 500 companies head-quartered there, and career potential for the ambitious.

If you reside within the confines of one of the cities noted here, you are off to a good start. If you don't happen to live near a city on our list, don't pack your bags just yet. Your successful career is not determined solely on the basis of geo-graphic location. Much is dependent on employers and op-portunity. As you explore the fast-track careers outlined in this book, we strongly recommend that you investigate both organizations *and* geographic areas that offer the best likeli-hood of success.

A FINAL THOUGHT

As you read through the remainder of this book we hope you will give serious consideration to more than the salary issue alone. Fast-trackers make big money not simply be-cause their title and field command it, but because they are *great* at what they do. In order to excel in a career you must love what you are doing, so remember to keep your interests and abilities in mind.

Finally, success is not just a one-shot deal; it is a full-time commitment. Remaining on top will probably take more en-ergy, time, and willpower than your initial achievement in getting there.

SUGGESTED REFERENCE BOOKS

The Almanac of American Employers
Jack W. Plunkett
Chicago, IL: Contemporary Books, Inc., 1985
Compilation of 500 of America's most successful corporations. Al-phabetical and industry listings. Information includes salaries, benefits, financial stability, geographical locale.

Book of American City Rankings
J.T. Marlin, et al.
New York, NY: Facts on File Publications, 1983

Breaking In
Ray Bard, Fran Moody
New York, NY: Stonesong Press, Inc. (Division of William Morrow & Co.), 1985

Over 500 of the nation's top corporate training programs with information on the employer, industry, training program, qualifications, recruitment/placement, salary benefits, and whom to contact.

County and City Data Book
Washington, D.C.: U.S. Government Printing Office, 1983

Everybody's Business
Milton Moskowitz, Michael Katz, Robert Levering
San Francisco, CA: Harper & Row Publishers, 1980

Detailed information on 317 of the nation's largest companies and descriptions of their corporate personalities. Includes company history, present operations, sales, profits, who's who, and more. (*Note:* Some information may be slightly outdated, but portions are still valid.)

Million Dollar Directory
New York, NY: Dun's Marketing Services, published annually.

The "Bible" of over 140,000 U.S. companies with net worths in excess of $500,000.

The 100 Best Companies to Work for in America
Robert Levering, Milton Moskowitz, Michael Katz
Reading, MA: Addison-Wesley Publishing Co., 1984

The authors attempt to identify the best employers in the United States. Book offers company profile and a rating system that keys in on pay, benefits, job security, chance to move up, and ambiance.

Ward's Directory of 51,000 Largest U.S. Corporations
Petaluma, CA: Baldwin H. Ward Publications, 1984

A listing of 42,000 of the largest privately owned companies and 8000 public companies. Firms are organized by location, sales volume, industry, and number of employees.

2

WALL STREET
Building a Career in Finance

"Wall Street has jobs for anyone who really wants one, regardless of how bad the market is or how many brokerage
firms have merged into nothingness."

—Cheryl Grandfield, 33,
current president of the
Women's Bond Club of New York,
in *Forbes*, May 6, 1985

Fast-trackers can appreciate the advantages of a financial career. Perhaps Wall Street, more than any other field, offers an
aggressive, high energy individual the fastest route to a six-
figure income. The very image of Wall Street conjures up an
image of excitement, frenzy, and risk. Since early in this
country's history, it has remained a sort of fantasyland where
fortunes are made as well as lost. There are "Wall Streets"
in almost every major American city, but New York's Wall
Street is the uncontested reigning champion. A financial-
district, is comprised of investment firms, brokerage houses
and exchanges—New York's "Wall Street" is host to the New
York Stock Exchange and the American Stock Exchange. If
you are an aspiring fast-tracker with a burning desire to
make it big among the Wall Street elite, you had better come
prepared for the toughest competition anywhere.

MANY APPLY, BUT FEW ARE CHOSEN ───────

It doesn't matter if your goal is investment banking, securities trading, or research—the fact remains, the financial community is an exclusive club and employers have their pick of the job market's creme de la creme. Recruiters and personnel executives at big name brokerage firms report that they receive a minimum of 250 unsolicited resumes weekly. At one investment bank there were over 1200 applicants for the firm's 25 new openings for the year.

We informally surveyed employers regarding the special skill requirements for this demanding industry. Their responses included the following traits:

Aggressiveness

Tenacity

Excellent negotiating skills

Decision-making capabilities

Ability to anticipate economic trends

Exceptional math aptitude

High stress tolerance

Willingness to devote long hours to the job

Stability—an individual cannot crack under pressure, even if a costly mistake has been made

Education is more crucial in the areas of investment banking and security or industry analysis; an MBA is practically (but not always) a prerequisite. High school and college graduates holding bachelor degrees fare better in positions in securities sales where verbal skills and strong selling ability are the two key ingredients. One recruiter at Salomon Brothers gave us her rules for reviewing resumes submitted for an entry level opening. (Remember, your objective in mailing a resume to an employer is to be granted an interview.)

Your resume must be easy to read with a logical progression of events.

- Keep the resume to one page maximum.
- Dates must be consistent.
- Typographical errors are an absolute taboo.
- Do not include a photograph of yourself.
- Omit hobbies and/or interests.
- Always submit a resume with an intelligently written cover letter.

The Salomon Brothers' executive added, "If you've been in the job market for several years, be selective about which past employers you choose to include. I'm not really interested in a minor position at Carvel! Also, if you walk your resume in, it may improve your chances of getting an interview."

At Morgan Stanley, one of Wall Street's biggest and most respected firms, we spoke with a personnel manager who specializes in the recruitment of financial analysts. The manager offered sound advice as well as a good perspective on hiring practices common to top finance houses.

Q: *Do you look for special degrees or majors from job candidates?*

A: No. There is no even distribution of degrees, although the bulk will be business related. I've seen graduates with concentrations in English, psychology, political science, and languages—all hired here at Morgan Stanley.

Q: *How many resumes do you receive on an average?*

A: The firm receives thousands of unsolicited resumes annually. Setting yourself apart from the masses is the trick.

A really good resume will demonstrate a solid record of achievement beyond academic accomplishment. I look for achievement both on and off campus. I want candidates who have exhibited *leadership*. That goes for the more experienced job applicant as well.

Q: *How many of your new analysts are hired through campus placement offices?*

A: The number of people we hire through unsolicited resumes is very small. We visit approximately ten to fifteen schools annually, usually in the fall and early winter. I would guess 95% of our new analysts come out of this campus recruiting.

Q: *What are some of the basic responsibilities of your new analysts?*

A: They'll be involved in data analysis, preparing various analytical statements as part of our overall presentations to clients. It is performing the analytical work that supports our client related activity.

WHO'S WHO

Prompted by this last answer, let's take a break for a question. Do you know the difference between a securities trader, a securities analyst, a stockbroker, an investment banker, or any of the other myriad of titles that filter through this industry? We would guess that you do not. For most people, there is real confusion when it comes to specific financial jobs and responsibilities. To many job hunters, the boundaries between sales, corporate finance, and investment banking are blurred. We've outlined various positions where people have found both fame and fortune; see which of these careers appeals to you the most.

Stock Exchange

A stock exchange is an auction-like setting where the American public can purchase shares in a corporation. The two most popular of these marketplaces are the New York Stock Exchange (NYSE) and the American Stock Exchange (AMEX), but there are eight other national securities exchanges and twelve commodities exchanges scattered throughout the United States. To do business on the floor of an exchange one must own a seat; an outside party may occupy one contracted from an owner. The NYSE (the nation's largest exchange) has 1366 seats and the AMEX 661. Buying a seat on the exchange is not an easy thing to do; in addition to meeting rigid industry requirements, one must come up with a hefty amount of cash—the current price of a seat on the NYSE is $480,000 and, on the AMEX, $175,000.

Brokerage Firm

In addition to the exchanges, Wall Street dealings include involvement with brokerage firms. A *brokerage firm* is a business that buys and sells securities for its customers. The brokerage house functions as a broker-dealer and is permitted to deal (buy and sell securities) with its own money or to act as a broker when the firm represents an outside party, receiving a commission for this activity. Usually, a brokerage firm owns one or more seats on the national exchanges so that it may do a heavy volume of trading.

Securities Sales—The Most Popular Path to Success

Let's look at career opportunities in securities sales. Most investors—whether they are individuals with a few hundred dollars or large institutions with millions to invest—call on securities salesworkers when buying or selling stocks, bonds, shares in mutual funds, or other financial products. Securities salesworkers are more commonly known as account executives or (stock)brokers.*

Account executives provide the means for an investor to buy or sell securities. They relay the order through their firm's offices to the floor of a securities exchange, such as the NYSE. If a security is not traded on an exchange, the account executive sends the order to the firm's trading department, which trades it directly with a dealer in the over-the-counter market.

Securities salesworkers also provide many related services for their customers. Depending on a customer's knowledge of the market, they may explain the meaning of stockmarket terms and trading practices; offer financial counseling; devise an individual financial portfolio for the client including securities, life insurance, tax shelters, mutual funds, annuities, and other investments; and offer advice on the purchase or sale of a particular security.

Securities salesworkers furnish information about the advantages and disadvantages of an investment based on each person's objectives. Some customers may prefer long-term investments for capital growth or to provide income; others might want to invest in short-term securities that they hope will rise in price quickly. The salesworker also supplies the latest price quotations on any security in which the investor is interested, as well as information on the activities and financial positions of the corporations issuing these securities.

Account executives may serve all types of customers or they may specialize in one type only, such as institutional investors. In institutional investing, most account executives specialize in a specific financial product such as stocks,

*Source: "Securities and Financial Services Sales Workers" as it appears in *Occupational Outlook Handbook*, U.S. Dept. of Labor, 1986–1987 edition. Bulletin 2250, p. 263–265.

bonds, options, annuities, or commodity futures. Some handle the sale of new issues, such as corporation securities issued to finance plant expansion.

Earnings

The biggest advantage of a career as a securities salesworker, or stockbroker, is the high income potential after a year or two of hard work in the field. The big money comes with institutional accounts, rather than those of individuals. Here again, however, the personality of the individual will determine the type of sales which will produce the right combination of satisfaction and monetary reward.

During training, new brokers remain on salary for a period of up to one year and go on straight commission thereafter. Beginning salaries range from $1200 to $2000 per month with the average being a $15,000 a year gross. The national average for stockbrokers is $78,000 annually, although those in major markets with institutional accounts earn upwards of $156,000. The industry's elite make anywhere from $300,000 a year to $1 million a year plus.

According to the Securities Industry Association, after candidates are licensed and registered, their earnings depend on commissions from the sale or purchase of stocks and bonds, life insurance, or other securities for customers. Commission earnings are obviously high when there is much buying and selling and lower when there is a slump in market activity. Most firms, therefore, provide salesworkers with a steady income by paying a draw against commission, that is, a minimum salary based on the commissions that they can be expected to earn.

An account executive will be expected to bring in at least $100,000 per year in commissions to the firm; the big name brokerage houses expect $250,000. The percentage of commission a broker retains varies in increased proportion to sales. For example, a broker bringing in $150,000 a year or less in commissions will keep approximately 30 percent of this figure, but at $1 million or more in commissions the percentage may rise to 45 percent.

The Wall Street tradition of rewarding high earners with hefty year-end bonuses is a practice that continues to flourish.

Best Locations

The top ten cities to settle in include (not in order ranking):

- New York (by far the best location)
- Los Angeles
- San Francisco
- Chicago
- Philadelphia
- Boston
- Atlanta
- Pittsburgh
- St. Louis
- Dallas

Getting Started

This is a career with a "survival of the fittest" theme. Twelve-hour days and longer are the norm with frequent weekend hours. The experts say that if you are hungry for riches and consider yourself "a street fighter" (industry slang), you will find your niche. Competition is stiff in securities sales. Interest in this profession has swelled due to a strong stockmarket and brokerage firms are hiring broker hopefuls at a furious pace. The majority of new hires enter the field between the ages of 25 and 35. The best possible way to get inside is by way of a successfully established contact who can refer you to those with hiring authority. A college degree is preferred (a concentration in financial or economic studies is noted with approval) and while an M.B.A. is a respected credential, it is not mandatory in sales. Because maturity and the ability to work independently also are important, many employers prefer to hire those who have achieved success in other jobs. Some firms prefer candidates with sales experience, particularly those who have worked on commission in areas such as real estate or insurance. Understandably, the overwhelming majority of entrants to this occupation transfer from other jobs.

It is several months before a new stockbroker has an opportunity to sell. It is necessary to pass a state licensing exam and gain full knowledge of the firm's products and services. (You must pass a specific securities exam to qualify as a stockbroker, but only those individuals sponsored by a brokerage firm may take the test.)

New brokers spend the bulk of their day on the telephone—employers expect them to make a minimum of 50 to 60 cold calls per day and the individual must produce rather quickly, opening 10 to 12 new accounts monthly. Industry experts estimate that the costs of training an entrant is the reason new recruits must prove themselves almost immediately. Many houses require the new employee to sign a two-year employment contract so that the company is assured some protection on their investment. As with most sales professionals, when brokers leave one firm to join another, they take their clients along and the firm suffers a loss of accounts. The two-year guarantee gives the employer the opportunity to get back a substantial return on its initial investment.

Building Client Accounts

Many securities salespeople begin their careers by cultivating friendships among attorneys, accountants, bankers, and anyone else who might serve as a possible source for client referrals—this process is called *influential networking*. They also scan the Yellow Pages for entrepreneurs with high revenue-producing businesses. Among the most popular are furriers, plumbers, building contractors, architects, health professionals, service station owners, restaurateurs, and morticians. We even heard of one resourceful beginner who diligently combed the newspaper's classified advertisements circling ads for anyone seeking to sell an expensive boat or car.

Eventually a broker is likely to specialize, dealing exclusively in stocks, bonds, mutual funds, government monies, stock options, or commodity futures. The principal form of advancement for brokers is an increase in the number and size of the accounts they handle. Although beginners usually service the accounts of individual investors, they may eventually handle very large institutional accounts such as those of banks and pension funds. Some experienced salesworkers become branch office managers and supervise other brokers while continuing to provide services for their own customers. Ambitious representatives advance to top management posts or become partners in their firms. One fast-tracker remarked, "If you haven't made partner within five years of entering the business, you're not really a Wall Street fast-tracker."

Training and Licensing

Securities salespeople must meet state licensing requirements, which generally include passing an examination and in some cases, furnishing a personal bond. In addition, salesworkers must register as representatives of their firm according to regulations of the securities exchanges where they do business or the National Association of Securities Dealers (NASD). Before beginners can qualify as registered representatives, they must pass the Securities and Exchange Commission's General Securities Examination, or examinations prepared by the securities exchanges or the NASD. Typically the exam(s) covers:

- Product knowledge
- Securities industry regulations and procedures
- Marketing procedures
- Brokerage office procedures
- Account servicing
- Economy and money markets
- Taxation
- Security analysis

Large national brokerage firms may require a second examination—the Uniform Securities Agents State Law Examination—that allows salesworkers to do business nationwide.

Most employers provide on-the-job training to help salespeople meet the requirements for registration. Because potential earnings are high in this occupation, competition for available training spots usually is keen. We learned that at one firm, candidates for stockbroker openings must go through a simulation training interview prior to being hired. During the session, applicants role play as brokers with simulated customers against the backdrop of hectic phones and the constant buzz of a stock quote machine.

In most firms, the training period is at least several months. Trainees in large firms may receive classroom instruction in securities analysis, effective speaking, and the finer points of selling. They may take courses offered by business schools and other institutions and associations, and undergo a period of on-the-job training lasting up to two years. In small firms, brokers generally receive their training in outside institutions and on-the-job.

Securities salespeople periodically take training, through their firms or outside institutions, to keep abreast of new financial products as they are introduced on the market. Training in the use of computers is important as the securities sales business is highly automated.

Profile

Joseph Kane, 30
1st Vice President, Dean Witter Reynolds, New York, NY

Joe Kane knew he wanted to work in the securities industry ever since his childhood, when he held a job delivering newspapers. One of his customers was a local brokerage firm, and that's where he got hooked. He financed his college education with early investments in the stock market. Today at 30, Kane ranks among the outstanding fast-trackers in his field. With a six-figure annual income, his own home in an affluent Connecticut suburb, and a new sports car, Kane seems to have it all, and he loves his job.

"People believe this job is easy, but it's not. The competition is keen, you are constantly second guessed by everyone, and the hours are long. I would guess there is a 50 percent drop-out rate over the first five years. The successful ones are ones who have the perseverance to work long hours, market knowledge, a thick skin, and can build trusting relationships with their clients."

At Dean Witter, Kane's responsibilities include developing portfolio strategies on investments ranging from purchasing stocks, bonds, mutual funds, to devising hedging strategies and very sophisticated tax shelters. "You need to be up to date on all new financial products, changing tax laws, and changing market conditions." Change is occurring daily and you must know how it will affect your clients and what strategies to counter with. Kane's clients are a diverse group of people, from prominent corporate executives, to professional athletes, small business owners and even medium-sized corporate pension funds.

"If you want to get into this field, my advice is to get as much sales experience as possible while you're under the age of 25. Try to position yourself so that you are selling to the rich in some sort of capacity. Brokering is a people business and you need to be able to develop instant rapport with someone new. You need to be tough . . . there's a lot of rejection before the success."

THE JOB OUTLOOK

The number of securities salesworkers is expected to grow faster than the average for all occupations through the mid-1990s. Most job openings, however, are expected to be created by those who transfer to other jobs, retire, die, or stop working for other reasons. Due to the highly competitive nature of securities sales work, many beginners leave the field because they're unable to establish sufficient clientele. Once established, however, stockbrokers have a relatively strong attachment to their occupation, both because of its high earnings and because of the considerable investment in training.

Employment of securities salespeople is expected to expand as economic growth and rising personal incomes increase the funds available for investment. As the baby boomers mature, they will enroll in pension plans, establish trust funds and contribute to the endowment funds of colleges and other nonprofit institutions. Industry personnel agree that even if the market plunges, job hunters should fare well in their area—many brokerage houses have committed themselves to long-term expansion and the development of product lines.

SECURITIES TRADER

The only way an individual can buy or sell securities on the floor of an exchange is by

1. owning a seat, or
2. having a contract to work someone else's seat.

A registered representative (or broker) can give the order to buy or sell, but it is the securities trader who executes the order. When you see newsclips or film scenes of the stock exchange, the frenzy and hub-bub that is apparent there is the daily workstyle of the trader. Men and women in this occupation spend their working hours bombarded with shouting, functioning amid chaos, and having to walk literally miles around the trading floor making deals. Industry personnel readily admit that it is a steady diet of pressure and tension, but it is also an environment in which some people thrive on the volume and sheer velocity of the work.

The trader's creed is, "buy low, sell high." What this means is that the trader makes his or her money on the "spreads"— the difference in the price the trader was told to pay and the actual price that was paid. Traders can specialize in one of the following four areas:

1. Floor members, also known as commission brokers
2. Specialists
3. Two-dollar brokers
4. Registered traders

Floor members work for one particular firm and follow through with the firm's orders to buy or sell specific stock, bonds, commodities, or currency. One firm may employ several floor members, depending on the number of seats on the exchange that the firm owns.

Specialists also work for a brokerage firm and handle assigned securities at designated trading posts on the floor. When a floor member receives an order from the house, he or she relays it to the specialist, who carries out the transaction. Specialists feel they have one of the most creative positions on Wall Street. A specialist must make quick decisions to act based on a judgment of the latest prices and bids to sell or buy. They have three key responsibilities:

- A specialist buys or sells at the customer's order and specified price. The specialist waits until the stock reaches the named price before acting. After carrying out the order, the specialist earns a commission on the sale.

- The specialist has been assigned specific stock, and must maintain an orderly market with it. This means that between trades, the specialist must take care that the price of traded stock changes in small increments so that investors feel their interests are being safeguarded.

- The specialist also develops an inventory of stocks based on a prediction of potential orders, risking his or her own capital in the belief that supply and demand will eventually balance.

Two-dollar brokers are not affiliated with any one firm. They wait for the floor to get "crazy" so that they can step in to handle the overflow from a brokerage house. In other words, so much is going on, the market is so active, that the two-dollar broker gets to do some trading because the firm's own traders are too busy to handle the volume of business on their own.

Registered traders own their own seats on the exchange, as well as their own inventory of securities. They buy and sell for themselves thereby amassing or losing their own fortunes.

This is the recommended best bet for those who really have capitalist dreams.

The training for these positions is essentially the same as that which securities salesworkers and analysts undergo; however, once training is completed, the trainee may request to be assigned to the trading floor. There is a system of apprenticeships employed both by brokerage houses and exchanges; it should be noted however, that many traders (particularly specialists) begin their careers as clerks for established specialists. Like salesworkers, traders eventually specialize and handle specific types of securities.

Earnings

The national earning average for traders is estimated to be $50,000 plus bonuses. Senior traders average $150,000 to $200,000 and the industry's superstars take home anywhere from $400,000 to $1 million dollars a year.

SECURITIES ANALYST

If you have excellent investigative skills and are good at research, an analyst position may be your best move. The securities analyst researches financial reports, reads trade journals of specific industries, analyzes statistical data and confers with top financial management at major companies. The main goal in studying these companies is so the analyst can recommend or reject projects that, after extensive analysis of potential profitability, would seem to help or hinder company growth. The analyst often participates in *divestitures* — the selling off or consolidation of unprofitable securities or divisions.

As an analyst you will fall into one of two categories: sell-side or buy-side. *Sell-side analysts* are employed by firms that sell their research to institutional investors, advising them as well as brokers and traders when and why to sell. On the analyst's part, selling becomes an integral feature of this job, since the analyst must convince corporate clients to buy the stocks that are analyzed. Sell-side is the more lucrative of the two areas because the analyst has the opportunity to generate a commission for their firm on the sale of a specific security. Sell-side analysts spend considerable time traveling and visiting various companys' plant operations to review the manufacturing process and to meet company management.

Buy-side analysts are employed by businesses that buy securities, such as insurance companies and investment banks. Their responsibility is to convince the principals of these firms to buy stocks with potential.

Almost all new analysts enter the field with an M.B.A. and/or an undergraduate degree in finance, economics, accounting, math, or statistics. The national earning average for securities analysts is $45,000 and up and senior analysts may earn $100,000 or more. For the most part, analysts are employed at straight salary plus a year-end bonus.

One organization which sponsors a program for training and certifying future analysts is The Financial Analysts Federation in New York City. It awards the Certified Financial Analyst degree (CFA).

INVESTMENT BANKING

Investment banking is a prestige business. More and more newcomers are attracted to this field because of the constant opportunity to interact with wealthy investors and the nation's biggest corporations. Investment bankers are on the inside of business's top money making deals. The banks themselves are located in large financial centers and serve as brokers and counselors on transactions for their clients. They earn their money by putting together a stock or bond deal (a fee is generated) and they make a commission based on a percentage of securities sold.

Investment bankers are best known as liaisons. Why? Let's say a corporation wants to issue new stock (or go public); the investment banker underwrites the offer, which means the bank assumes liability and also finds prospective buyers for the shares. If all goes well, everyone (the investment bank, the corporation, and the shareholders) earn money. If the deal goes sour, the investment bank ends up owning the client's stock.

Investment banking is a rather small, exclusive circle populated by fewer than 10,000 members. *Money* magazine (December 1986) reports that rookies in the field typically earn $97,500. Industry predictions say that an investment banker breaks into a six-figure income three years after earning a graduate degree, and after five years in the business he or she is earning close to $250,000.

The following seven firms are the powerhouses of investment banking. Each has headquarters in New York City and also has offices around the country.

Drexel Burnham Lambert
60 Broad Street
New York, NY 10004
212-480-6000

First Boston
Park Avenue Plaza
New York, NY 10055
212-909-2000

Goldman Sachs
85 Broad Street
New York, NY 10004
212-902-1000

Merrill Lynch Capital Markets
1 Liberty Plaza
New York, NY 10080
212-637-7455

Morgan Stanley
1251 Avenue of the Americas
New York, NY 10020
212-703-4000

Salomon Brothers
1 New York Plaza
New York, NY 10004
212-747-7000

Shearson Lehman/American Express
American Express Tower C
World Finance Center
New York, NY 10285
212-298-2000

FINANCIAL PLANNER

This job title is unique in that it can encompass virtually everybody in the financial arena. The use of a financial planner has grown tremendously in popularity, thanks to the average consumer's interest in his or her financial future. A planner considers a client's overall financial situation and then makes recommendations as to distributing income, planning for the future (retirement and estate planning), tax strategy, and making wise investments.

A planner makes a written plan for each client and is compensated by a fee and/or commission. Currently there are no formal training requirements for entering this profession, nor is a professional certificate mandatory. Certification similar to an accountant's CPA status is possible; there is the Certified Financial Planner (CFP) and the Chartered Financial Consultant (CHFC).

One very popular program is available at the College for Financial Planning in Denver, Colorado, which offers the CFP and other assorted financial degrees. The college is an independent, nonprofit educational institution that has graduated over 8500 candidates since its incorporation in 1972. An excerpt from their 1985 Bulletin reads:

> By the year 2000, financial planning will have become a middle-class phenomenon. The predicted demise of Social Security for retirement purposes, the increasing tax burdens of the two-income family, the effects of inflation and the growing complexity of financial products and services are some of the factors that will motivate Americans to seek the services of a financial planner.

If these ideas have stirred your interest, consider this as well: Financial planners currently average $53,000 annually, and over 60 percent of those in the field are earning over $80,000 a year.

GLOSSARY

Bond:
A promise from either the government or a corporation to repay the loaned money given a lender on a specific date, with the agreement to pay a named rate of interest until the date comes due.

Broker:
An individual with the authorization to represent another individual or party in a financial transaction, and who is compensated for this service with a commission.

Brokerage House:
A financial firm that acts as a broker and/or dealer in securities.

Dealer (Trader):
Person authorized to buy and sell securities.

Investment Bank:
The business of underwriting and distributing corporate securities.

Portfolio:
A pool of money in the form of cash and/or securities, invested with the prospect of earning a specific rate of return.

Registered Representative:
Individual authorized to act as a broker and/or dealer for a brokerage firm that is a member of a stock exchange.

Securities:
Evidence of ownership or money owed (stocks and bonds are securities).

Spread:
The difference between the bid and the selling price of a security.

Stock:
Shares of ownership in a corporation.

WHAT YOU SHOULD BE READING

American Banker
1 State Street Plaza
New York, N.Y. 10004
212-943-6700

Barrons National Business and Financial Weekly
22 Cortlandt Street
New York, N.Y. 10007
212-285-5243

The Directory of Exceptional Stockbrokers
Published annually by the Hirsch Organization
6 Deer Park Trail
Old Tappan, N.J. 07675
Profiles the nation's 125 top stockbrokers

Forbes
Forbes, Inc., 60 Fifth Ave
New York, N.Y. 10011
212-620-2200

Fortune
Time-Life Building, Rockefeller Center
New York, N.Y. 10020
212-586-1212

Investor's Daily
150 Broadway, Suite 811
New York, N.Y. 10038
212-964-7380

Money
Time-Life Building, Rockefeller Center
New York, N.Y. 10020
212-582-1212

Standard & Poor's Stock reports on 3500 companies
25 Broadway
New York, N.Y. 10004
212-208-8000

The Wall Street Journal
22 Cortlandt Street
New York, N.Y. 10007
212-285-5000

ORGANIZATIONS FOR MORE INFORMATION* ─

American Association of Financial Professionals
Box 1928
Coco, Florida 32923

Financial Analysts Federation
1633 Broadway
New York, New York 10019

International Association of Financial Planners
5775 Peachtree Dunwoody Road
Atlanta, Georgia 30342

National Association of Securities Dealers, Inc.
2 Broadway
New York, New York 10004

New York Futures Exchange
20 Broadway
New York, New York 10004

*Career information also may be obtained from the personnel departments of individual securities and brokerage firms. In addition, always write for a firm's annual report and descriptive brochures before exploring career possibilities with the organization.

New York Institute of Finance
70 Pine Street
New York, New York 10270

New York Stock Exchange
Education and Training Division
11 Wall Street
New York, New York 10005

Securities Industry Association
120 Broadway
New York, New York 10271

(There is a $1 charge for this material.)

3

ADVERTISING
Making the Product Sell

Oh, What a Feeling!
Don't Leave Home Without It
Have It Your Way
Plop, Plop, Fizz, Fizz
You've Come a Long Way, Baby

These one-liners *make* successful advertising campaigns. Not only could most of us identify the product these phrases sing about, but we could sing along in cadence.

With 95 billion dollars spent annually in the United States alone to promote products, services, and organizations, you can imagine that we consumers are bombarded at every turn with well-planned, creative, snappy, memorable advertisements. Advertisements invade every aspect of our lives. Through repetition, careful manipulation, and brand identification, we buy soap powder, headache medicine, and blue jeans. Who are the people responsible for performing such powerful hypnosis on us—where and how do they do it?

Advertising: The pace is fast, the action exciting. The responsibility and rewards are great. Young people who demonstrate excellence are rewarded with six-figure salaries, big bonuses, expense accounts, and a fast-track to the top. Several of the advertising executives we spoke with agreed they could spot a fast-tracker within three years of his or her first job. Advertising is definitely a young person's field. And if you make it, you can be rich by the time you are 30!

Fast-trackers work hard, meet the right people, and take advantage of opportunities or make them for themselves. Above average performance moves them ahead quickly toward their long-term career goals.

WHY ADVERTISING?

Advertising is the business of helping other businesses and organizations sell their product, idea, service, or image. In 1905, marketing theorist John E. Kennedy said, "Advertising is salesmanship in print." This is still true today, with the addition of the broadcast media. Further, it is advertising that helps stimulate business growth and serves to maintain the competitive marketplace so important to keeping our economy strong.

Advertising is the nation's largest service business. The service it performs is clear and simple. It helps the client achieve market growth. Creative people, salespeople, and business people combine their efforts toward this goal.

Advertising is a sales job. The whole effort is to sell us on, or to get us to buy the service or product. The premise of a good advertising campaign is:

- To convince the consumer that the product is the best.
- To point out and create a need for the product or service.
- To improve the organization's image.
- To attract attention.

Effective advertisements must be:

- Simple and easy to understand
- Truthful

- Informative
- Sincere
- Attention-Getting

The effective advertising person must be clear-thinking and have a natural insight into what motivates the consumer. The advertising agencies seek to hire smart, talented, inquisitive people who thrive on challenge and take pride in providing creative solutions.

HOW TO PREPARE FOR AN ADVERTISING CAREER

A college education is virtually essential for success in advertising. We learned, however, that an advertising major was generally *not* the favored degree among the upwardly mobile. Liberal arts majors fared much better; in fact, a liberal arts degree was held by more than one-half the fast-trackers we spoke with.

At the entry level, the sought-after skills include strong language and math ability, as well as typing. The "Madison Avenue" set display qualities not unlike those needed to succeed in any other business. Those that excelled in advertising did have certain characteristics in common:

- Strong interpersonal skills
- Leadership ability
- Self confidence
- Clear thinking
- Strong imagination/innovative mind
- Drive
- Initiative
- Energy, energy, . . . and more energy.

Be willing to start at the bottom and work your way up. On the account side there is no substitute for on-the-job training. On the creative side, your portfolio is the key to your success—you either have it or you don't. At Grey Advertising, where the emphasis is on "home grown" talent, most of its senior management have worked their way up through the ranks.

GETTING IN THE DOOR

Advertising is a *highly* competitive field.

1. Utilize the Standard Directory of Advertisers known in the industry as "The Red Book." This book lists all the agencies, their size and which accounts they handle. Familiarize yourself with the agency, then apply for the job.

2. Follow the want ads, read trade journals such as *Advertising Age* (the industry bible), published by Crain Communications to know which agencies are landing new accounts. It follows that where there are new accounts, there are probably new jobs. Also, register with your state employment services office and private employment agencies.

3. Use direct mail, but contact *a person*, not a personnel department.

4. Contact anyone you know in the advertising business for leads and an introduction. Develop a network of advertising professionals by joining professional organizations. See the list of these organizations at the end of this chapter.

5. Keep your resume concise and to the point. Include a hard-selling cover letter to set you apart from the crowd. It is your cover letter, not your resume, that should be different enough and persuasive enough to convince the employer to see you.

6. Consider that persistence, timing, and luck are all factors in your job search.

7. Follow your instincts and grab opportunities as they arise.

8. Always send a "thank you" note after an interview. So few people do this that it really sets you apart from the crowd.

Remember, the hardest part about fast-tracking in advertising is getting your first job.

While large agencies offer the greatest opportunity for growth (tracking), smaller agencies offer the beginner the widest exposure to advertising as a whole. And this is an advantage: the more you know, the more you'll grow. The account executives and the creatives in a smaller agency usually "wear many hats" in order to satisfy all the needs of the client. This allows for more hands-on experience and greater responsibility sooner.

However, it is important to note that today, the prestige and big financial rewards that come with working for a large agency, on one of the top packaged good accounts, out-weigh the opportunities afforded by smaller agencies. So, it is okay to learn at a smaller agency, but if you dream of reaching advertising stardom, move to a large, full service agency early in your career.

Are There Any Training Programs?

At most agencies, training is on-the-job. According to a survey conducted at the 16 largest U.S. advertising agencies by *Advertising Age* "Training is widespread in media and account management but minimal in research and creativity." Though some of the agencies do have formalized training programs, the majority that we surveyed offer controlled, on-the-job training in which a new recruit works closely with a supervisor.

Aside from learning good business practices, the new recruit or entry-level person is expected to learn the client/ agency relationship, the relative values of print and broadcast advertising and how to select the right vehicle; how the media department plans and buys; and the bottom line of course, developing and presenting the product in a cost efficient way.

One agency that does offer a rather specialized and extensive training workshop to a highly selective group of advertising professionals is Young & Rubicam. Twice a year, Young & Rubicam's New York headquarters welcomes top-ranking professionals from around the world into their "Advertising Skills Workshop." This month-long intensive training program takes the participants through each operating department of the agency so that they come away with a true understanding of the agency network.

For entry-level positions, agency recruiters tell us they look for detail-minded candidates with strong language and math skills. Typing is an added plus and may actually aid you in securing a position. Jill Novorro, a vice president of the New York based Katz Independent Television, tells us she carefully watches the progress of her entry-level staff, who are sales assistants, moves them ahead when appropriate and makes sure that their salaries reflect their achievements.

Understanding the Agency Network ───────────

There are four functioning arms of an advertising agency. They are:

1. Account management
2. Media/research
3. Creative services
4. Office administration/finance

At the time the agency agrees to represent the client's product, three department heads (accounts management, media and creative) combine their efforts to formulate an advertising plan or campaign. Their goal is to define:

- An advertising concept
- A time schedule
- A budget

Then each department assumes the appropriate responsibility and each department head delegates the assignments to his or her staff. Finally, office administration/finance oversees that the budgets are adhered to, that the work flows easily and without hitch from department to department, and that projects are completed on time.

An advertising agency earns its income from commission on advertising placed by their clients. The advertising costs the client the same whether placed through an advertising agency or directly with the media. However, there may be additional costs to the client for the planning, creative, and production work done by the agency.

Within the various divisions, we've chosen to include titles where fast-tracking is possible.

Accounts Department

This department is responsible for dealing with the client in all aspects of the campaign. It is the most visible and sought-after department. Let's examine some positions within this framework.

Accounts Manager/Supervisor. Responsible for overseeing and guiding the course of new business and accounts and supervising the management of existing accounts by working with a staff of account executives. Helps create budgets and project schedules, initiates projects, develops advertising strategies, and oversees the work of account executives. Answers to the board of directors or agency president. Six-figure salaries are commonplace at this level of management.

Account Executive (AE).   As a liaison between client and agency, the account executive meets client needs. Part of the job entails winning prospective accounts, as well as maintaining good relations with existing accounts. The account executive works directly with the brand or product manager on the client's side, is responsible for day-to-day business needs, and acts as liaison between the various departments of the agency. This is a high-visibility position, and good account executives advance quickly, but there is a high turnover as accounts succeed or fail. A good account executive is a valuable agency asset; as a result, performance incentives and bonuses are granted in accord with the person's track record. Senior account executives earn $50,000 a year or more, including bonuses, expense accounts, and other perks. Superstar salaries could be as high as $100,000 or more.

Assistant Account Executive.   A training-ground position to develop skills necessary to be an account executive; provide support to the account executive; looks after the loose odds and ends of the supervisor's efforts; a "prove yourself" position. Starting annual salaries average $15,000–$18,000 and can reach $60,000–$80,000 or $100,000 (through promotions) in just a few years.

Media/Research Department

This department is responsible for market analysis, consumer research, production evaluation, and ultimately for providing the data and statistical insight to create an advertising campaign.

The Market Research department conducts studies designed to show who the buyers are for a product and how they react to the product, its packaging, and price. They are also responsible for assessing whether the advertising campaign gets the message across to the buyers and motivates them to buy the product.

Marketing Manager/Media Director. Responsible for supervision of staff, planning, and scheduling; authorizes the purchase of air time on television and radio or newspaper and magazine space for ads; usually works with account executives and clients to develop ad plans. Answers to agency president and/or board of directors. Salaries for department heads often are $125,000 a year, and more.

Media Planner. Initiates market research and/or advertising studies. Analyzes the data given by clients and aids the account team in planning the campaign. Here salaries rise along with experience. Starting salaries are $25,000–$35,000 a year. Also the visibility in this job often leads to quick promotions.

Media Buyer. Negotiates and procures time and space, deals with media representatives, evaluates and selects media markets (networks, regions, programs) to suit a campaign. Salaries are similar to those in media planning, although planners often make more money and climb up the ladder faster.

Research Director. Responsible for the accumulation, preparation, and presentation of research findings, statistics, and market analysis data to marketing and accounts staff (and occasionally to the client). Supervises and assigns research staff projects. This is upper management and it is rewarded with salaries of $70,000–$80,000 and sometimes $100,000 or more.

Research Analyst/Market Researcher. Analyzes existing markets and projects market potential; advises media and creative staff on ad choices; provides statistics on the consumer, general economics, and the marketplace. Salaries range between $14,000 and $40,000, depending upon experience.

Media Researcher. Analyzes media options, then suggests most effective media to sell the product; projects media trends. Commonplace salaries for beginners are $14,000–$18,000 and as high as $40,000 depending upon experience.

Creative Department ────────────────────────

The creative department is the most diverse, complicated and pressurized arm of the agency. Its goal is to create, design and produce advertising art and copy.

Creative Director.   Responsible for all copy, art and production work; works with marketing and accounts director to formalize ad concept; guides department staff to meet goals. An extremely prestigious position compensated with salaries of $100,000–$150,000 and more, plus expense accounts, bonuses, and a corner office.

Copy Supervisor/Group Head.   Supervises writing staff, develops ideas with art director, writes copy and creates central ideas to be written out in detail by copy staff. Offered here is $75,000 + annually, and a fast-track to creative director.

Copy Writer.   Writes advertising for print media, scripts for radio and television commercials, and sales promotional material for sales department. An idea person. He/she has to write words that sell. Talented copywriters can earn six figure salaries.

Art Director.   Coordinates the efforts of the Account Executive, art staff and copy writers to produce ad art, storyboards (for television commercials), magazine layouts and other visual media. A mid-level management position can offer a salary of $65,000–$75,000 annually.

Commercial Artists, Designers, and Production Staff.   Perform the actual drawing of ads; design and layout of ad pages; works with photos, copy, and other visuals to create ad. Competition here is stiff. Entry-level salaries are low $13,000–$16,000. However, earning potential is great and is limited only by your talent and salesmanship.

Production/Advertising Assistant.   Gal/Guy Friday with general office skills. This position offers opportunity to learn print, TV and/or radio production. Entry-level growth spot. This foot-in-the-door opportunity offers lots of exposure, little prestige, $15,000 to start but *lots* of potential.

Profile
Lois Block, 38
Freelance Producer, New York, NY

After graduating from high school, Lois Block got a degree from New York University Film School gearing herself for a career as a filmmaker. Through an internship, Block landed her first job as a "gofer" in a small filmmaking company. Within a year she worked her way up into casting. Sounds glamorous, we thought. "Boring" she said. "It was not film-making." She joined McCann Erikson as a young producer and immediately began overseeing the production of commercials from storyboard to film. She tells us she worked on the Bahamas Ministry of Tourism account and was "always tan." Glamorous we thought. "Hard work and long hours," she said. While some people were thinking about their jobs, she was thinking about her career. Young and Rubicam was her next stop, where she became an executive producer.

Experience taught Block how to visualize the story on film, knowing how it should look in order to get the client's message across. Known for her style and quality, Block went out on her own. "I never thought I couldn't make it. I've always felt if there's a mountain, climb it."

Office Administration and Finance Department

This department is responsible for the inner agency workings, and for billings for agency services. It oversees total agency expenditures and maintains budgets. While positions in this area are *never* fast-track, they offer an individual an opportunity at least to enter the field. We learned that media buyers, art directors, and market researchers rarely make it to the top. We encourage you to pursue your advertising career in either *account management* or *copywriting*.

Please note that job titles may vary from agency to agency. What we tried to do here is to give you an overview of the agency network. For specific information on job titles pertaining to a particular agency, please refer to the personnel department at that agency.

We also learned that the best paid people in advertising may be the freelancers or the independents. One young woman, 37 years old, told us that in six weeks she makes what she earned for the entire year when she started her advertising career 15 years ago. She hires herself out on a per-project basis, often as a consultant. Not only can she choose the projects she works on today, but she has more leisure time than other fast-trackers she knows who earn less than she does.

More Than Just TV Commercials

Television is the most used, most effective, and possibly the most expensive medium for advertising. Unlike radio listeners, who may study, work, or drive while listening to the radio, or newspaper readers who may listen to the radio while reading, television viewers usually give the "tube" their undivided attention.

Television enables the advertisers to show their products in action and to demonstrate their use. Television is *the* mass medium—it reaches 98 percent of the households in the United States. The average household watches about $6\,^3/_4$ hours of television each day. That's a pretty large buying public. Television advertising accounts for an average of 80 percent of all of the advertising dollars spent. You say glamour industry, we say big business.

Please refer to the chapter on Media for a full discussion on television.

MARKETING IN ADVERTISING

In creating an ad, the advertising group (the account executive, the creative manager, the product or brand manager on the client side, and all support) must consider the product, the price, the channels of distribution, and effective promotional outlets.

Marketing plays a major role in their plans. The advertising group must also consider what promotional vehicle or combination of selling tools will yield the greatest buying response. This is called the promotional mix and it is what makes up the selling and marketing strategy. Selling tools can include point-of-purchase displays (POP), coupons, premium offers, special deals, demonstrations, and trade shows.

While there are several classifications into which all advertisers fall—industrial and business advertising, trade advertising, and more—we chose to explore the kind of marketing in advertising that affects the general public, that is, consumer advertising.

An effective ad can mean the difference between success and failure for the product, as well as for the advertising group. The millions of dollars that national advertisers spend to promote a product is mind-blowing. According to *Advertising Age*, Gillette spends 20 million dollars trying to persuade the consumer to buy Good News Razors®; Del Monte spends 8.5 million dollars promoting Hawaiian Punch®; and Proctor & Gamble spends 16.7 million dollars "convincing" us to buy Camay®.

Advertising is not a science. But marketing techniques, surveys, interviews, taste tests help guide the advertiser into the market where their product might have the most appeal. Market researchers evaluate the product, the target group, and the media in order to advise the account group what will yield the most successful return on available advertising dollars. We found that the most widely liked commercials don't always generate the most sales. We learned that the success of advertising is affected by changes in consumer tastes, social and cultural differences (demographics), economics, technology, and the actions of the competition. Advertising *is* a competitive business. The advertiser is indeed competing for *your* business. Therefore, a good promotional campaign should inform, persuade, and influence behavior.

We can see that marketing techniques aid the advertiser by providing insight into what people buy, what product, at what price, and how to persuade those consumers to buy their product. If you have a mathematical mind, like research and statistics, marketing in advertising might be an area for you to explore further.

WHERE ARE THE JOBS?

Of the people working in the advertising field, about one-third work for agencies. Of these, more than one-half are employed in New York, Los Angeles, and Chicago. The other half work for independent or branch offices all over the United States. New York City has traditionally offered the greatest opportunity for those who want to make it to the top fast.

About two-thirds of the people in advertising are not in agencies. They may work for:

- Newspapers, selling time or space to advertisers
- A manufacturing company or bank or corporation, as a brand manager, copywriter or art director
- Direct response/direct mail agencies
- Printer or engraver
- Market research services
- Freelance
- Advertising agency
- In-House agency

Some of these positions are self-explanatory; others, such as copywriter, have already been covered. Let's look at a few of the nonagency jobs.

- *Direct Response.* Any form of advertising done in the direct marketing form. Uses all types of media, direct mail, catalogues, circulars, brochures, the telephone. Direct response is a selling strategy that by-passes retail channels.

- *Direct Mail.* One form of direct response advertising, direct mail, represents the third largest share of the advertising marketplace, after television and newspaper advertising. Flexibility and selective advertising are the key to direct mail advertising. Direct mail offers the flexibility to reach a pre-arranged targeted group of consumers and the means to select when and how to reach them. Selectivity in this case means with a minimum of waste. Through market research and list buying, the direct mail advertiser increases the probability that the consumer who gets the advertising circular, catalogue, brochure, or leaflet *is* a potential customer.

- *Market Research Services.* Provides the advertiser with calculated insight into who the buyers are for their product; the reason they may buy this type of product; and how they react to the product, its price, and its packaging. It also tries to determine whether the advertising message gets the consumer to buy the product.

THE TOP TEN U.S. ADVERTISING AGENCIES ——

1. Young & Rubicam
   285 Madison Ave.
   New York, NY 10017
   (212) 210-3000

2. Ogilvy & Mather
   2 E 48 St.
   New York, NY 10017
   (212) 907-3400

3. Ted Bates Worldwide Inc.
   1515 Broadway
   New York, NY 10036
   (212) 869-3131

4. J. Walter Thompson
   466 Lexington Ave.
   New York, NY 10017

5. Saatchi & Saatchi Compton Inc.
   625 Madison Ave.
   New York, NY 10022
   (212) 754-1100

6. BBD&O (Batten Barton Durstine & Osborne)
   383 Madison Ave.
   New York, NY 10017
   (212) 415-5000

7. McCann-Erickson
   2185 Lexington Ave.
   New York, NY 10017
   (212) 697-6000

8. D'Arcy Masius Benton & Bowles
   909 Third Ave.
   New York, NY 10020
   (212) 909-9451

9. Foote, Cone & Bellding
   101 Park Ave.
   New York, NY 10178
   (212) 970-1000

10. Grey Advertising
    777 Third Ave.
    New York, NY 10017
    (212) 546-2000

Source: Crains' *New York Business,* December 1986/January 1987, Volume II No. 52

While all of these agencies are headquartered in New York (some with large offices in Chicago), it is possible that they maintain a branch office closer to your home. You needn't begin your career in New York, but you must be prepared to move to New York early in your career to earn big bucks.

KEEPING PACE WITH ADVERTISING

The world of advertising is ever-changing. Even as we researched this chapter, accounts went from one agency to another; jobs (big jobs) were lost to the merge purge; and mega mergers were happening as larger agencies continued to gobble up smaller ones in an effort to win and keep big companies and big corporate clients.

The mega mergers of the 1980s saw Ted Bates swallowed by Saatchi & Saatchi. Benton & Bowles align itself with D'arcy, MacManus, Masius and BBD&O merge with Needham Harper Worldwide. The mega mergers we speak about permit instant growth into specialty areas of advertising (i.e., direct marketing, promotions, transit advertising) but mostly they open the door to an international marketplace. In some instances these mergers simply permit the agency to be competitive in this expanding marketplace where millions of advertising dollars are at stake.

We learned:

1. Consumer advertising is on the rise in foreign countries.
2. International or multinational companies prefer to do business with one agency that can service their domestic *and* international advertising needs as well as perform a wide range of marketing functions (again, direct marketing, promotions, etc.).

GLAMOUR AND THEN SOME

Advertising conjures up images of glamour, bright lights, and big money. In truth, the advertising business is a high-stress, roll-up-your-sleeves business. There is no doubt that burnout plays a major role in keeping advertising a young person's field. The pace is *fast* and because of that fast pace and because of the pressure, people do not work a lifetime in a large advertising agency. Instead they either opt to open their own shop or go over to the client's side where the pressure is less frantic.

The fast-track to the top often requires you to travel in the fast lane. Late night parties with the right people and pressure, pressure, pressure—to create and generate new and exciting ideas within a specified time. Working hours are often irregular and it is not uncommon for advertising executives to work evenings, weekends, or holidays in order to complete an assignment on time. One fast-tracker told us, he "does work long hours, but never more than 24 in one day."

Profile

Michael Solow, 32
Vice President/Creative,
Durfee, Solow, Roth Advertising, New York, NY

Michael Solow's real passion was writing. But he graduated from Vassar with a teaching certificate because he thought it was more practical economically. While at school he founded the Vassar Chronicle, a popular magazine. After a year as a private school teacher, he set aside the teaching certificate and took a job as an editor of a small town magazine.

In 1979, he decided to return to New York. Combining summer agency experience, business savvy, and his innate writing ability, Solow worked his way up to his present position.

Solow tells us that to be successful in the creative area, one must have a good dose of self-confidence and the ability to take criticism. "You must be able to have your ideas rejected and come back with an even better idea." He says further, "Although writing ads takes creativity, it is commercial creativity. I think people who come into advertising having deep creative aspirations have a problem. It's not your own personal work. It's creativity, but in a business context. There are very defined limits. You're expressing a client's point of view. Yes, there's a lot of room for creativity, but you're not necessarily expressing your own point of view about the world necessarily. After all, advertising isn't art—it's selling."

"It's not easy—it doesn't just come. Advertising takes a lot of hard work. It's deceptively easy-looking. You have to understand, there are many factors that go into the making of an ad, and many demands. Demands from the client, pressure from your own supervisors who have a certain view of what should be done. At its best, it can be a very satisfying partnership."

Solow continues, "Indeed, you are a salesperson, but your tools are a television commercial or a print ad, not face to face. So in a real sense, your persuasion job is that much harder. That's why the creative element is so critical."

On success in advertising Solow advises anyone interested in the creative side of advertising to put together a portfolio from a good course in writing ads and remember that quality is better than quantity. And finally, "Your portfolio is your resume."

EMPLOYMENT OUTLOOK

Because advertising is a sales vehicle that must always be new, fresh, and relevant, and because advertisers are always looking to appeal to the consumer's pocketbook, it is likely that the advertising industry as a whole will continue to prosper. With the introduction of new and sophisticated advertising media—cable, home videos, shop-at-home television hours, and TV auctions, to name a few, we are certain opportunities prevail and big bucks will continue to await the innovative, creative, hardworking advertising professional through the end of this century and beyond. It is important to remind yourself of the volatile nature of the business. The loss of a big account can mean major layoffs, even for the most talented.

Onward and Upward

The biggest and most prestigious accounts at the agency are packaged goods accounts (i.e., Proctor & Gamble's Crest® Toothpaste, Del Monte's Hawaiian Punch®, Bristol Meyers' Excedrin®, General Foods' Jell-O®). If you are offered a job working on a fast food, pharmaceuticals, financial service, automobiles, communications (i.e., phone or alternative mail), airlines or computers account, grab it.

So then, advertising is your career choice. You are determined to begin either on the account side or the creative side, depending upon where your talent lies. (Remember, these two areas are usually the fastest track to the top.) You know now that time spent working on a packaged goods account will probably speed your ascent. You are willing to put all your effort, time, and just a little less than your whole being into your career. One successful woman summed this up for us. She said of her career, "I'm putting in the time (sometimes 12-hour days, weeks at a time) to make as much money as I can, and then I'm going to get out while I'm still alive." (She will retire to the beach house she built in the Hamptons, probably before she's fifty.)

Set your sights high, work hard and smart, think success (a little luck helps), and you too could find a rewarding career in advertising.

GLOSSARY

AAAA:
American Association of Advertising Agencies. Established 1917, a review board and an agency supported, industry governing force.

Boutique Agency:
A small agency that offers advertisers very creative but sometimes limited services.

Campaign:
An advertising effort that is planned for, and conducted over a specific period of time.

Client:
A company or the organization that buys the services of an advertising agency.

Demographics:
Characteristics of a population including sex, age, income level, and other statistical data into which people can be separated.

Direct Advertising:
A message that is delivered directly to prospective customers by the advertiser.

Direct Mail:
Circulars, catalogues, brochures, leaflets and other printed material sent through the mail to prospects selected by the advertiser. It accounts for the third largest share of advertising investment dollars in the United States.

Full-Service Agency:
Organization that provides complete service for advertisers—copywriting, art, market research, media analysis, scheduling—and the services of the creative people in producing print advertisements, radio and TV commercials.

Marketing Research:
A systematic seeking out of facts related to a specific marketing problem.

NARB:
National Advertising Review Board—A board of 50 members established in 1971 by the advertising industry to police deception and eliminate bad taste in advertisements.

Point-of-Purchase Displays (POP):
Promotional advertising aimed at reaching you at the retail outlet. Displays in the supermarket at the front of the aisle represent a fine example of an effective POP tool.

Premium Offers:
Merchandise that is offered in addition to advertiser's product to attract and sell people who do not usually buy the advertiser's product or who do not buy it very often.

Promotional Mix:
The combination of advertising, publicity, personal selling, and sales promotion that a company chooses in order to increase its profits.

Target Market:
The part of the total market comprising the most likely prospects for a particular product, those with a need for a product, a willingness to buy it, and the ability to pay for it.

WHAT YOU SHOULD BE READING

Advertising Age
740 Rush Street
Chicago, IL 60611

Advertising News of New York (ANNY)
230 Park Avenue
New York, NY 10017

Adweek
230 Park Avenue
New York, NY 10017

Adweek/Art Directors' Index
820 Second Avenue
New York, NY 10017

Ayer Directory of Publications
NW Ayer & Sons, Inc.
West Washington Square
Philadelphia, PA 19106

The Creative Black Book
Friendly Publications
401 Park Avenue South
New York, NY 10016

Leading National Advertisers
Advertising Age
740 Rush Street
Chicago, IL 60611

Madison Avenue
750 Third Avenue
New York, NY 10017

Standard Directory of Advertising Agencies
(The Red Book)
National Register Publishing Company, Inc.
3004 Glenview Road
Wilmette, IL 80091

Television/Radio Age
1270 Avenue of Americas
New York, NY 10020

ORGANIZATIONS FOR MORE INFORMATION ——

The Advertising Council
825 Third Avenue
New York, NY 10022

Advertising Research Foundation
3 East 54 Street
New York, NY 10020

Advertising Women of New York
153 East 57 Street
New York, NY 10022

American Advertising Federation
1400 K Street NW
Suite 1000
Washington, D.C. 20005

American Association of Advertising Agencies (AAAA)
200 Park Avenue
New York, NY 10017

American Marketing Association
230 North Michigan Avenue
Chicago, IL 60606

Business Professional Advertising Association
205 East 42 Street
New York, NY 10017

Direct Mail Marketing Associations
6 East 43 Street
New York, NY 10017

Institute of Outdoor Advertising
485 Lexington Avenue
New York, NY 10017

Television Bureau of Advertising
1345 Avenue of Americas
New York, NY 10019

Women in Communications, Inc.
150 West 52 Street
New York, NY 10019

4

MAKING IT
IN THE MEDIA
Communicating for a Living

Gal/Guy Friday. Major network seeks ambitious college grad for diverse entry opportunity. Work in sports production/broadcasting. Work w/directors, producers, writers. Go on assignment at sports events. Must be willing to work hard, wear many hats & possess limitless energy. Highly visible spot w/promotion possible if you can thrive in chaos. Journalism, communications, English grads welcome. Must type 50 wpm and/or be familiar w/personal computer. Send resume to . . .

More than 77 percent of all adults read a daily newspaper. Nearly 99 percent of all American homes have at least one radio. And 96 percent of all American homes have at least one television.

These media provide us with virtually all of our entertainment and news information. At the flick of a wrist we can tune into our favorite music, see the latest news report, or scan the local newspaper advertisements for the best sales.

Mass media—newspaper, radio, and television—influence every aspect of our lives from what we *think* and *know* about world events, to the food we eat, the music we prefer, and the style in which we live. Because of mass media, we know about warfare thousands of miles away; we can see and hear Pavarotti as he performs at La Scala in Milan, Italy; we can even watch a mother giving birth on public television. Often, media provides an escape from the pressure of ordinary living. It also provides companionship. We live in an era shaped largely by the opinions, sights, sounds, and values presented to us by the media.

Media that reach large numbers of people are called *mass media*. While books, magazines, and film are all vehicles of mass communication, for the purpose of this book we will be focusing on those media which operate largely at no cost or minimal cost to the consumer.

- Newspaper
- Radio
- Television

The basic responsibility of mass media is to present to its audience the highest quality entertainment and the most accurate and clear portrayal of an event or happening.

We offer you a formula for fast-track success in this field. We recognize that while this formula could be generic and apply to all the fast-track careers we cover, we choose to include it in this chapter because of the extreme competition for jobs in this industry. The formula is as follows:

1. *Network.*   Make yourself visible at professional association meetings and conferences. Volunteer to assist with committee assignments and special events.

2. *Read.*   Learn all you can about the field. Borrow and subscribe to trade journals and industry reports.

3. *Volunteer.*   Become involved in civic or cultural functions. You will have fun and gain insight, experience, and an opportunity to rub shoulders with CEO's and key decision makers.

4. *Collect samples.*   Compile and keep adding to a portfolio that shows the extent of your talent. Put together only the samples of your work that represent your best efforts. Quality makes a better impression than quantity.

5. *Be well-groomed.*   First impressions count, so look your best at an interview.

6. *Prepare.*   Before an interview, research the organization and the position that is available. The quality of your questions about the organization and about the position available can give the interviewer insight into your potential. Be prepared to take the initiative in describing your qualifications and what you believe you can accomplish in the position.

7. *Persist.*   Be your own best friend, don't begin to doubt yourself or your abilities. If you don't get one job, try for others.

8. *Think positive.*   Take your commitment to work in your chosen field seriously. Interviewing and accepting rejection are not easy but both are valuable learning experiences and will serve as dress rehearsals for the right interview—the one that will lead to your dream job.

GETTING STARTED

Start with a deep commitment and a love of media. Focus on which form of media—print, radio, or television—you want to fast-track your career. A college education is a major plus and technical know-how is essential for all technical jobs within the industry.

Although available positions are far short of the number of applicants, keep in mind that the world of communications is expanding rapidly and making increased use of technologies like satellite and cable systems as well as newer and more sophisticated ones. We will examine some of these later in this chapter as alternative career opportunities.

Your first job is relatively unimportant. *Take anything* — getting your foot in the door is what counts!

As in any job search it is important to do your homework on the firm to which you are applying and the position involved. We have included at the end of this chapter a list of reference books and trade journals that will be informative and may be helpful to you in your job search. Consider that an entry-level job titled, "Gal/Guy Friday" might give you the perfect opportunity to get into this very competitive, glamour-filled industry. A "Receptionist" might really be a production trainee in disguise. Examine each job opportunity for its long-range potential. Consider what you can learn and whom you can meet. Network! This is an industry where a friend of a friend is the single best way of landing a job.

Several broadcast executives we interviewed were asked to list in order of importance what areas of knowledge might help a prospective employee get ahead. They were:

- Sales
- Programming
- Broadcast journalism
- Station management
- Research ability
- Typing

If you have any of these skills and/or college coursework in these areas, a job in media could be waiting for you.

Media Impact

Ninety-six percent of American homes have at least one television (1 percent higher than homes having indoor plumbing!). The average household watches six and three-quarter hours of television each day and/or listens to the radio three and a half hours a day. Some of our children are being raised by television. Many children begin regular television viewing by the time they are two or three years old. A new generation of media professionals must be committed to providing programming that is informative, entertaining, and educational. Although newspaper and radio are losing popularity, they remain an important source of both entertainment and information to the masses.

What is being printed and broadcast is important to how we perceive ourselves and the world around us. Be forewarned—this "glamour" industry demands commitment and perseverance if you intend to make it to the top. The competition is stiff and potential fast-trackers come from all over the country to try their hand at making it big time.

ALL THE NEWS THAT'S FIT TO PRINT

The Past

Newspapers were perhaps the first organized form of mass communication. As early as 1600, some effort was made at printing and distributing newspapers. By the 1830s mass-circulated newspapers took hold. The latter part of the nineteenth century saw a period of expansion and growth for the newspaper industry. The newspaper not only became a mass medium—it had also become big business. Newspapermen like William Randolph Hearst and Frank Gannett built financial empires from the papers they published.

The Present

Today, newspapers are a way of life. For millions of Americans, the day begins with the newspaper and a cup of coffee. Newspapers offer something for everyone—local and world news, stock prices, sports, crossword puzzles, classifieds, advice columns, birth announcements, comics, and much, much more. The greatest appeal of newsprint is that readers can read it at their own pace and read only what interests them. Each newspaper reader is his or her own editor. While broadcast media has a limited time in which to present the news, and must concentrate on items that will be of interest to the greatest number of listeners or viewers during their limited on-air time, the newspaper can present a more complete accounting of the day's events and in vivid detail.

The Newspaper from the Inside, Out

At the head of all the paper's operations is the publisher or general manager, who may or may not own the newspaper, and who usually does not run the day-to-day operations. Under the publisher's authority are the editors, the business manager, the mechanical superintendent, and their staffs.

The editor, also known as the editor-in-chief, oversees the production of all primary news as well as the editorial opinion of the paper. Since this position is the heart of a good newspaper, it is a most important post, which brings with it considerable prestige and generous compensation.

Reporting to the editor-in-chief, is the editor of the editorial page, who represents the newspaper's stand or its point of view. This is expressed through editorials, letters to the editor, and political cartoons. Also reporting to the editor-in-chief is the managing editor, who supervises a host of assistant editors—news, sports, home, food, etc. The editor's function is to determine what is newsworthy.

Working for the assistant editors are reporters, researchers, and writers. They are assigned stories according to the editor's news plan. For example, the city desk covers local news of a general nature except sports and society news. The sports editor and society editor handle coverage in their respective areas. State, national, and international news are provided largely by wire services. The wire editor monitors the stories that come in and selects those judged most interesting and important to the paper's readers. Further, special editors, depending on the newspaper's needs, handle a variety of topics—farming, mining, whatever is of special interest in the area.

The copyediting staff checks stories for accuracy, punctuation, spelling, and grammar. The headline writer summarizes in a few words the essence of the story in order to capture the reader's interest.

Also reporting to the publisher is the business manager. The business manager has three important functions:

1. Producing revenues
2. Getting the newspaper distributed
3. Handling routine business affairs

Each of these areas is staffed by executives responsible to the business manager.

The advertising manager not only produces advertising content but sells advertising space. This department is the major source of revenue, and the profit arm of the newspaper. In fact, about 65 percent of newspaper content is advertisements. Advertising sales is often overlooked as a fast-track media alternative because it is not a "creative" area. However, we learned that sales offers top salaries and a fast-track to upper management.

The circulation manager oversees that the newsstands and coin racks are stocked and, more important, oversees home delivery—usually two-thirds of the paper's daily circulation.

Finally, the job of the mechanical superintendent is to get the newspaper printed and out on time. Newspapers do their own printing, with a staff of typesetters and printers. Most writers now use computer terminals instead of typewriters, so that the copy is recorded, transmitted to the copyediting department, and composed into galleys, all electronically. The galleys are prepared for printing directly on the computer terminal.

Big Papers, Small Papers

Those of us who live in big cities think of newspapers in terms of the major metropolitan "dailies," *The New York Times, The Los Angeles Times, The Miami Herald,* and *The Chicago Tribune,* to name a few. According to the Accrediting Bureau of Circulation (September 30, 1986), *The New York Times* has a circulation just over one million daily and *The Chicago Tribune* has a circulation of 750,000. Although these are a dominant part of the newspaper industry, they are not representative of your typical daily paper. In contrast, according to the American Newspaper Publishers Association, the major trade association, the average daily has a circulation of between twelve and fifteen thousand. In fact, 85 percent of all dailies have less than fifty thousand circulation.

The Wire Services

While local news, photographs, and feature stories are produced by the local staff with some larger dailies having correspondents in the field, the major source of state, national, and international news is the wire service. There are several, but the Associated Press (AP) and the United Press International (UPI), are the most influential news-gathering sources in the world. The media as a whole relies heavily on these wire services.

A wire service is a news-gathering organization of reporters (correspondents) operating out of news centers or bureaus in the United States and in foreign countries. These reporters and photographers feed stories and pictures into the bureau, which in turn sells them to the local newspaper or broadcast medium. The average newspaper contains more news from wire services than from its own reporters. The next time you read a newspaper, notice the origin of the stories you read; you may be surprised how many stories originate from the wire services.

The Weekly Press

Weekly newspapers, or community newspapers as they could appropriately be called, publish in and around small towns and suburban areas. There are four times as many "weeklies" published as dailies and that number would be more than five times as large if we included ethnic, special interest, or free circulation publications.

The focus of a weekly newspaper is the local community. Weeklies do not attempt to compete with the daily newspapers but rather to fill some important gaps. The purpose is to inform its reading public of news about the local church, the local school, the reader's city and county government, local sports, and local sales.

Weekly papers are as personal as the guy next door; and indeed the "newsworthy" are likely to be friends and neighbors. Weekly newspapers are supported by the local advertisers whose ads reach the segment of the population most likely to patronize the store or service.

Could you begin here? Perhaps. Use your local experience as a springboard to a fast-track career with a larger daily newspaper.

Feature Syndicates

Feature syndicates provide local papers with comic strips, cartoons, crossword puzzles, word games, household tips, syndicated columns, i.e., Dear Abby, Miss Manners, Jimmy Breslin, and daily horoscopes. These regular newspaper features are sold to and published by newspapers nationally. No newspaper could afford to hire individual writers to develop these areas; and no newspaper would be complete without them. The features editor allocates space and chooses what his or her readers will read.

EMPLOYMENT OUTLOOK

It is important to note that the newspaper industry ranks as the third largest employer in the country. Newspaper profits continue to be healthy and actually outpace the profit margin reported by most other businesses. Because they are profitable to run, newspapers generally offer a stable work place.

Although the broadcast media has taken away some of the newspaper industry's readership, the need for print media remains strong. In print, complex issues can be developed and defined at length. Different angles can be explored without wasting expensive on-air broadcast time. The product is timely and portable and one can read and reread the newspaper anywhere, and be well informed.

Newspapers not only employ a large number of people but also a good variety of talent. Because there are so many different kinds of newspapers published, the opportunity for fast-tracking in the newspaper industry abounds. We encourage you to explore the printed media for these career opportunities.

Earnings Overview

We found the earning potential varied considerably, depending on the size of the newspaper and its geographic location. Writers and editorial assistants might expect to earn $20,000 to start. Senior editors and experienced reporters could earn $60,000–$70,000 plus, and on large circulation newspapers $100,000 plus per year was average for senior editors and "superstar" reporters.

Syndicated columnists can earn six-figure incomes. In addition, many writers and editors supplement their salaried income by doing freelance work.

BACK TO THE FUTURE OF RADIO

By 1915 technology was developed to permit regular commercial broadcasting. And by 1930 radio as a source of entertainment became a major part of American culture. During the 1930s and 1940s, radio programming began to respond to the growing interest of the public—the need for *more* and *varied* shows. Coverage of big sporting events, drama, comedy, and variety shows were added to the musical format already popular with the fast-growing listening public. Broadcast journalism (news reporting) followed bringing the events of the world right into our livingrooms.

Radio's heyday lasted for about a quarter of a century. In the late 1940s television made its appearance and people thought radio was doomed. So radio, as a matter of survival, underwent a revolution. First, its programming expanded and, second, transistors made radios portable.

No other medium beats radio in providing the public with up-to-the-minute information, fast-breaking news reports, and round-the-clock programming. Radio shows no signs of waning in popularity and, in fact, it is as popular today as it ever was. Most of us awaken to a blast from the radio, we listen to our portable Walkmans as we travel to and from work, at the beach, and in the car. Indeed the listening public must like what it hears on radio—we tune in more than three and a half hours each day. Rush hour or "drive time" in radio jargon (6 AM–10 AM, 4 PM–7 PM), provides the most concentrated listening audience and valuable advertising dollars. Thousands of commuters, on buses, trains, and those stuck in traffic find radio a relaxing companion.

Programming, Audience and Ratings, or Who Listens?

Radio broadcasting exists solely on the basis of its advertisers. The strength of this media lies in its ability to provide a well-defined audience. A station develops its audience by its chosen format and the personalities of its on-air staff.

Radio subscribes to a rating service in order to prove its share of the audience. Each percentage point represents thousands, possibly millions of advertising dollars. The audience profile helps advertisers buy time only on stations whose profile is close to that of their potential customers. Further, knowing not only the number of listeners but the composition of listeners helps the station to program for their listening audience. Of course, good ratings create prestige as well as profits.

Radio advertising is surprisingly inexpensive. Fees vary widely depending upon the station, the program, and the time of day.

WHO'S WHO

Radio stations come in many sizes and, while the number of employees vary, the staff functions are the same. A typical small town station may have ten to fifteen employees; a large station in a metropolitan market may have two or three times that many.

There are four primary functions carried out at the radio station, they are:

- Sales
- Programming
- Engineering
- General administration

All four department heads report to the general manager or station manager, whose job it is to run a successful business. Not only does the station manager need to be knowledgeable in all phases of studio operations, he or she must also be a good business person.

The sales manager (often the second highest paid member of the staff) supervises salespeople who solicit local advertising. Contrary to the way the average listener perceives radio, it is *not* the disc jockey who is the most valued asset but rather the sales staff or account executives. (At small stations, the disc jockey or announcer or other staff members may double as salespeople.)

Closely related to the sales department is the traffic department, which schedules commercials and other programming. The traffic department keeps a "traffic log" or "listing" by broadcast time of the exact time that each commercial is to be played or read. These commercials must be carefully placed so that a commercial for shaving cream is played during an early morning sports round up and not at 10 AM when the listeners are mostly housewives. Further, the traffic department is responsible for seeing that competing sponsors are not aired back to back. The local Coca Cola bottler would be unhappy if the announcer completed his sales pitch, and started in with a sales pitch for some other soft drink.

Programming

The programming director supervises the station talent, public service segments, music, and other programming. He directs the preparation of broadcast material and oversees everything that goes on the air. The disc jockey and/or the station announcer report directly to the program director, as does the news department, if the station has one. (On many stations, the wire service provides nearly all the news.) In fact, the program director serves the same role as the editor-in-chief of a newspaper, determining all programming except the commercials. Once again, in small stations where the staffers wear many hats, the station manager may perform this function.

Engineering

The chief engineer and his assistants keep the station on the air. They also maintain and repair the equipment so that on-air time runs smoothly.

Administration

Like any business, a radio station requires basic administration. This area includes all support functions from the personnel director to the accounting staff; from the general manager to the secretaries. Administration should not be overlooked as an entry-level career opportunity.

EMPLOYMENT OUTLOOK

While radio no longer fills the same need it did in the 1920s and 1930s, it certainly has a strong foundation in our culture. It is still the most versatile, adaptable, and efficient of all media. We think its appeal will never be replaced by television or cable because it will continue to provide up-to-the-minute news, music, and timely talk shows in its ever-portable, hardly distracting way.

The *Occupational Outlook Handbook* (1986–87) assures us that though competition for jobs in broadcasting in general will be keen, it will be easier to get a job in radio because radio stations hire more beginners. Many of these jobs will be at small stations where the pay is relatively low. We suggest you learn all you can about the varied jobs in radio and move to a larger station where the pay is better. It is necessary to know that the larger stations "pick and choose" and primarily seek to employ only experienced personnel.

Earnings Overview

Salaries vary widely, depending on the type of station, the market it serves and the location. In general, larger radio stations pay better than smaller stations. The sales staff is consistently well paid regardless of location. Overall, the salaries of announcers or disc jockeys was not impressive but the top 10 percent, those fast-track professionals we are interested in, do earn $60,000 or more. And indeed, the superstars are very well paid.

What attracts fast-trackers to radio broadcasting? Some like the idea of becoming a national personality whose name and voice are known to many. Others are attracted by the income levels of some top executives. Whatever your attraction may be—radio lives!

THE BIRTH OF TELEVISION

Television was born in America in the late 1940s and it changed the lifestyle of the American people. At its introduction television was regarded with suspicion. In 1939 *The New York Times* ran this blurb about television,

> The problem with television is that people must sit and keep their eyes glued on a screen—the average American family hasn't time for it.

By the 1960s, television had come of age. It had grown into a very profitable business—one that provided advertisers with the largest audiences the world had ever known. Here again, the sale of commercial television time is what supports television programming. The advertisers actually pay for our viewing time.

Television brings the world into our livingroom, for 75 percent of us, in living color. Via satellites, we are able to experience the jungles of Africa or Christmas at the Vatican while remaining in the comfort of our own homes. We learn to love and hate by what we see on the "tube." We know which products keep us smelling nice, which airline is taking us to more places, and which soft drink tastes better according to the latest taste tests, . . . and we buy it. Television, which appeals to more of our senses than any other medium, is the most powerful and influential of all media.

THE WORLD OF TELEVISION

If you think your fast-track personality could best serve the television industry, explore with us these opportunities. The most lucrative areas of this mega business are:

- Networks
- Independent stations
- Cable and satellites

Networks and Their Affiliates

The majority of commercial television stations in the United States are affiliated with a network. To be affiliated, the station must agree to broadcast a specified number of network programs and is compensated for providing its time and service. Further, multiple stations simultaneously receive and transmit the same program and commercials, enabling viewers from California to Maine to watch the same programming. The national advertiser likes this because they only need to buy one spot which will be viewed on all network affiliates throughout the country. The major commercial television networks are CBS (Columbia Broadcasting System), NBC (National Broadcasting Company), and ABC (American Broadcasting Company). All three networks are headquartered in New York. Each maintains branches and studios in other large cities around the country.

Independent Television Station

The television station that does not have a network affiliation is known as an independent station. It buys television programming from various syndicators and/or produces its own programming. The independent leases or buys many motion pictures originally shown in movie theaters, re-runs of programs previously shown on network affiliated stations, and first-run productions too. The independent television station can provide an excellent training ground for a career in television broadcasting.

All commercial television stations—independent and network affiliates—are required by the FCC (Federal Communications Commission), the regulatory arm of commercial television, to broadcast at least 28 hours a week. The majority of stations are on the air many more hours than this, some around the clock.

Cable Television and Satellites

Technically, cable is simply another method of television distribution (or delivery). Since 1949, cable has provided television reception to rural, hilly, and mountainous areas across the country where airwaves would be interrupted by the terrain. Today, what cable television represents is a greater choice of programming services.

It is only in the last ten years that the cable industry, with the help of satellites, has become a growth industry. With the effective use of communication satellites (used to transmit signals around the world), we can view not only selected programming but world events—the royal wedding or the disaster at Chernobyl. Thanks to satellites, distance is no longer an obstacle for television and cable. While some think the cable boom is behind us, we think the opportunities in cable and beyond are enormous. The Department of Labor foresees an expansion in the number of job opportunities in the cable industry and states that although the greatest growth seems to have been experienced in the early 1980s, cable promises to continue to be a growth industry in the coming years.

KEEPING PACE

We think it is important for the fast-tracker interested in a career in broadcasting to consider that television is a youthful industry and that cable television is still in its infancy. New and sophisticated technology will continue to expand and change our television viewing habits. We suspect there are areas yet unexplored or, at the very least, underdeveloped.

We learned that the cable industry at this stage in its development has a continuing need for marketing and sales experts. Also that bright, enthusiastic, and innovative financial people, administrative people, producers, and engineers are all welcome to apply.

WHO'S WHO

Every station, network affiliate, independent or cable system generally has three key managerial positions, they are:

- General manager or station manager
- Sales manager
- Program or production manager

The General Manager or Station Manager ─────────

This is the business side of television, with responsibility for accounting and business decisions. The general manager is the top administrator at the television station. He or she sets the policies and establishes guidelines for the station's staff. The station manager also consults with all department heads on a regular basis; represents the station in the community and at industry meetings and represents the station in relations with the FCC. If this sounds like a responsible job, it is! The general manager oversees the station's operating budgets which could represent millions of dollars. It is the station manager who makes long-range plans and strategic decisions.

Extensive experience in broadcasting and years of business experience are prerequisites to this management job. The general manager may receive a flat salary, or a combination of salary and bonus based on the profitability and efficiency of management performance.

Sales Manager ───────────────────────────────

The sales manager supervises the salespeople who sell commercial advertising time. The sales staff provides the income that pays the station's bills and produces a profit. We remind you that television is *not* the glamour industry so many fantasize it to be, but rather a business where billions of advertising dollars are at stake. Be mindful that there are eight to ten minutes of advertisements broadcast every viewing hour. Is television advertising big business? You bet it is!

Staff salaries vary according to market size, but the generally well-paid salesperson or account executive earns $50,000 plus, with salaries two and three times that in the major markets such as New York, Los Angeles, and Chicago. A station's salesperson's potential earnings are limited only by the effort put into the job and the ability to sell. The sky's the limit.

Profile

Jill Novorro, 32
Vice President, New York Sales Manager,
Katz Independent Television, New York, NY

A college graduate with a masters in Rehabilitation Counseling, Novorro sort of "fell" into advertising and sales. She began her rise to the top ten years ago, working for a small advertising agency in an entry-level capacity. Recognizing that the area she liked best was television sales, she wasted no time acquainting herself with people in the industry. "Television is lively and fast paced, and I knew that was where the money was," she tells us. She also knew it would take time and so she developed a plan and worked out a career strategy, which included a move to a larger agency.

At Ted Bates (a top ten agency), she went from a junior media buyer to a buying supervisor in just three years. She admits she did well but says, "I was earning pennies compared to what I felt I could potentially earn."

As a buyer, Novorro met fast-tracking salespeople and resolved to become one of them. "It wasn't easy," she tells us. It took her one year of persistent pitching to get into the company she's with today. "They turned me away numerous times. They told me there would never be a position in the company for me since I lacked sales experience. My biggest frustration was how to gain sales experience if no one gives you your first start. One day one of the chiefs took me to lunch and he said, 'Jill, we've become friends since you've started pitching the job, take it from me, go look elsewhere.'" Surprisingly enough, weeks later, Novorro was hired as a full-time salesperson. The company had been gaining many new clients and they decided to add her to the staff—Novorro's persistence paid off.

"They just put me out on the street and said 'sell.' No training. I have to admit that it may not be the best way of doing it. It was a difficult transition for me. I was on my own. I knew what transpired between buyer and salesperson, but I didn't know the relationship with the client on the other end. I knew my relationship with the buyer who bought the time, but I didn't know what my relationship was supposed to be like with my client, the TV station. I made some mistakes. If you know how to deal with people and you work hard, and you ask questions, you learn enough. Obviously, I learned quickly, because within a year and a half I was promoted into a sales management position, and in this business, that's unheard of! People wait years to become a sales manager in spot television sales."

Novorro has experienced minimal sexism in her fast-track career. "I'm a money-producing person, not a money-producing woman. Once you start producing for people, all of a sudden your sex is of no importance to them. You're a person that is a profit-making machine. Never hold anything back because you're a woman. If anything, it's an advantage."

For Novorro, the rise to the top has had its rewards, but not without sacrifice. She works long hours, sometimes until nine or ten o'clock every night.

Of success she says, "If you want something bad enough, apply yourself and don't give up."

Program Director

The program director selects and develops the broadcasts for the station and oversees the budget and production. The producers and directors of each show are responsible to the program director who reports directly to the station manager.

Once again, station and market size factor into potential earnings. The larger the market, the greater the earning power. Independent stations generally pay better than network jobs because they do more of their own programming. Often the director is also the producer.

Producer

The producer is responsible for seeing that the program, commercial or scheduled on-air event goes as planned. Duties include planning, determining format and executing live or taped productions. The producer oversees the talent, script, sets, props, lighting, sound, and budget. He or she must be knowledgeable in all phases of basic studio production. The producer might earn $1000 per week or $1000 per show, depending on talent and demand.

Although we won't detail the job particulars of the technical staff, we mention them because without the technical expertise of these people—the camera crews, tape editors, and audio and visual directors—there would be no picture or sound on television. These technical specialties are generally union jobs; the members receive union wages and benefits and overtime.

News Director

The news director is responsible for the image, format, and content of all news broadcasts, reporting to the general manager of the station. The news director acts as editor-in-chief in the newsroom, hires and fires personnel, makes duty assignments, and coordinates the gathering and reporting of news by the entire staff. Energy, imagination, and lots of ideas about what will make a good news story are requisites. For successful news directors handsome remuneration is offered—often six-figure salaries and all the trimmings.

News Producer

The news producer decides on the order of presentation (the "line-up") for all stories. It is the news producer's job to check all details before air-time and be responsible for any on-air adjustments. In New York, Chicago, and Los Angeles, the producers of the evening news can earn $70,000–$80,000. An executive producer can earn $80,000–$100,000 and more.

News Editors and Writers

This staff member edits all copy and writes all necessary transitional copy to keep the show moving. Not a big money job, but puts you in contact with the right people. This is a good position for a fast-tracker to move through.

News Desk Assistant

This Gal/Guy Friday is responsible for fielding incoming calls from the public, the press, and the public relations people. The news desk assistant checks the newswires and distributes the copy to key newsroom personnel. Here again, the pay is low but the chance to network your way around the newsroom makes this a sought-after opportunity.

The Newscaster or Anchorperson

This is perhaps the most coveted job in news broadcasting. The anchorperson's main functions are to host regularly scheduled newscasts, report some of the major news stories, provide lead-ins for other stories, and to serve as a representative personality for the newscast. Aside from a pleasant appearance and clear speaking voice, the newscaster must have a thorough knowledge of all news developments. A number of years of newsroom experience generally precedes on-air reporting. Newscasting is an attractive job and is often considered the height of a television reporter's career.

Salaries vary widely, depending on the market. Superstars like Barbara Walters and Dan Rather earn over a million dollars a year, and anchorpersons are often paid $150,000 to $350,000 or more per year.

The job titles and functions listed above are simply an overview of who and what it takes to operate a broadcast system. There may be jobs we did not include in this overview that may be more specific in nature. To learn more about this sort of job opportunity, please refer to your library.

ALL THAT GLITTERS . . .

Basically, the "glamour" of broadcasting is somewhat mythical; staff members at all levels do a lot of routine work. Keep in mind that radio and television stations are "for-profit" operations and each department is responsible for turning its share of the profit. Willingness to take a job where one is available—in a small town instead of New York or Los Angeles—and a willingness to start at the bottom may make the difference between success and failure in breaking into the world of television.

WHAT'S IN IT FOR ME?

Competition for entry-level positions is tough. There are more qualified applicants than job openings. Often, starting salaries are below those starting salaries in other industries. But the fast-tracker who is willing to start at the bottom and work up the ladder will find that broadcasting offers job security, excellent pay (beyond the entry-level), and pleasant surroundings.

A survey of broadcasting employees conducted by the National Association of Broadcasters and the Broadcast Education Association concluded that nine out of ten staff members are satisfied with their working conditions, wages, and fringe benefits. Salaries are generally good for all types of broadcasting positions and excellent for key performers and executives. Generally, television pays better than radio; larger stations pay more than smaller ones; and commercial stations out-pay educational and public stations.

Again, broadcasting is a relatively young industry and new technology is constantly being developed in an effort to provide even more sophisticated equipment, programming, and broadcasts. We feel there will continue to be new and exciting avenues in the broadcast media for the fast-track professional to explore.

Profile

James Stolz, 31
Senior Producer, Special Projects, WCBS TV, a division of CBS, Inc., New York, NY

When James Stolz graduated from Vassar (1976), he wanted to be an actor. Today, he is a producer with a top network.

After college, Stolz opted for a career in the theatre. He tried acting for four or five years, and although he appeared in several off-Broadway shows, he felt unsure of his success. Stolz felt he always had the ability to create his own opportunities and his next move was into print media. He used his hometown newspaper experience in an effort to propel his journalistic career. Unfortunately for Stolz, the print media was experiencing some lean years and Stolz found few opportunities for a staff position with a major New York paper.

Stolz's career change from print to broadcast journalism demonstrates his "take the bull by the horns" attitude. He explains, "I thought I was interested in television news, so I came to CBS. They had a job opening as a producer for their investigative unit on Channel 2 (WCBS local news in New York City). And I said, 'Hey look guys, I've written about 300 articles for New York City newspapers and magazines. I know a lot about the city. I'm a good reporter, but I don't know any television at all. I haven't the faintest idea how you do what you do, but I'm willing to make a trade. Basically, you teach me TV and I'll share my knowledge of New York and my skills as a reporter.'"

CBS bought the idea and Stolz was hired. He started in the investigative unit, moved up to the "writers pool" and now, only three and a half years later, is the Special Projects Producer for Channel 2 News.

Stolz loves his work. He works on the "long, urban features," chooses many of his stories himself, writes, films, and helps edit them. Unlike the majority of people in television, Stolz does not worry about ratings. He concerns himself instead with putting the best stories in New York City on the air. "That's what I like to do, so that's what I really do well," he said in explaining his philosophy.

Like every fast-tracker we spoke to, Stolz's work is his number one priority. He's there when he's needed and, more often than not, he's there before 9 AM and he's still there well after 5 PM. Stolz feels that writing ability is the most important talent needed for anyone trying to break into network news. Intuition is another "must" characteristic. He explains, "You just have to have a good sense of what's news. You have to have a good sense for truth, you must have integrity; and a sixth sense about what concerns people in their daily lives."

GOOD PUBLIC RELATIONS FOR PUBLIC RELATIONS

So you never thought of public relations as a mass medium. Although public relations is not a media vehicle like newspaper, radio, or television, it is considered a mass medium in the abstract. It "uses" mass media in order to promote its product. The job of the public relations person or firm is to inform, publicize, promote, lobby, identify issues, assess attitudes, and monitor change, all in the client's best interest.

The public relations person is a communications expert, who earns a fee by securing and maintaining a favorable public image for the client. Good public relations usually finds its way into the media, but in some cases, good public relations keeps the client out of the media. Occasionally, public relations can save face. Read on . . .

In the recent past a few Extra-Strength Tylenol® capsules were found to be laced with cyanide. The press ran the story on front pages all over the country—bad press for the makers of Tylenol, Johnson & Johnson. To the credit of the company's public relations people, Johnson & Johnson did not try to avoid or ignore the problem, but acknowledged it, withdrew the product from the market and began rebuilding its image—all in a few hours. Good public relations strategy saved the reputation of a star product and managed to avert what could have been a publicity disaster. So sometimes the best public relations involves checking or limiting the damage of negative media exposure.

Can I Make It?

When we asked several public relations executives to list for us the personality characteristics of a successful public relations person, this is the summary of the traits stated most often.

Those most likely to succeed in this competitive industry are those who are:

- Hard working, with a good sense of timing
- Perfectionist

- Excellent with written and oral communication skills
- Curious
- Enthusiastic and enterprising
- Flexible and energetic
- Persistent, persuasive, and diplomatic
- Tactful
- Self-effacing

The field of public relations is not for the applause seeker. The best public relations is undetectable and the best public relations people stay behind the scenes. But this field is not for shy people; it's for assertive people who are not troubled by rejection.

Today most sizeable organizations have one or more individuals assigned to a public relations function. Not only in business and industrial firms, but also in educational, religion, military, entertainment, and sports organizations, you will find a press agent. Last but not least, government makes extensive use of information specialists to disseminate news and information to the public directly and through mass media.

In fact, the government is the largest employer of public relations people in the United States, followed by the nonprofit sector and the corporate world. Aside from the obvious public relations functions of media exposure and talk show interviews, writing corporate newsletters, and preparing annual reports are also public relations responsibilities as are many other activities.

Getting Started

A college education combined with any media experience is excellent preparation for public relations work. Extracurricular activities, such as writing for the school newspaper or a local publication, or an internship in public relations can be the leading edge when competing for entry-level positions. Membership in the Public Relations Society of America may allow someone interested in breaking into this competitive industry to make valuable professional contacts. We learned that newspapers are a good training ground for future publicists and that writing talent is essential to success in public relations.

When applying for a job in public relations, your resume is your press release. It should represent you well. The style is as important as the content. Zero in on results. Be prepared to start anywhere, even as a secretary. One public relations executive suggested that the public relations professional gets paid for four things—time, work, experience, and contacts. Since newcomers to the field don't usually have the experience or contacts, they can only offer the willingness to put in lots of time and hard work to gain experience and make the contacts. Above all else you must feel that you would rather be doing public relations than anything else!

What's In It for Me?

According to the *Occupational Outlook Handbook* (1986–1987), employment of public relations workers is expected to increase faster than the average for all occupations throughout the mid 1990s. The opportunities are great because virtually every store, company, restaurant, political figure, celebrity, and organization uses publicity to promote good will and to generate visibility. Given that we live in an image conscious society it seems safe to say that public relations will remain an important growth industry.

Salaries of $70,000, $80,000, and $100,000 plus, attract fast-trackers to this industry. A good reputation and a proven record of success can carry with it the title of "vice president," an office with a view and all the frills.

GLOSSARY

ABC:
American Broadcasting Company. One of the three major television networks.

Affiliate:
A station that has contracted to carry certain programming from a programming service.

CBS:
Columbia Broadcasting System. One of three major television networks.

Cable System:
A business designated by a local municipality to distribute signals of television stations and other television services to households that pay fees for such service. Cable TV systems transmit programming to television sets via coaxial cables.

Disc Jockey:
A radio entertainer whose program consists of a chosen format. Disc jockeys play records and tapes.

FCC:
Federal Communication Commission. A governmental agency that regulates the cable and broadcast industries.

Independent Stations:
Stations owned and operated by private individuals or corporations.

NBC:
National Broadcasting Company. One of the three major television networks.

Network:
A group of broadcast stations, usually affiliated by contract although some may have common ownership.

Rating:
The size of the audience viewing a particular program, expressed as a percentage of potential viewership.

Satellite:
A device orbiting the earth that receives and transmits signals.

Syndicated Column:
A supplement edited and printed by a publishing company which provides it to noncompeting newspapers.

Wire Service:
A syndicated process of transmitting news information by telephone, telegraph or wireless. "Wire Service" as used in connection with the news media are organizations. AP is a wire service, UPI is another.

WHAT YOU SHOULD BE READING —————

Television

Billboard
Billboard Publications, Inc.
One Astor Plaza
1515 Broadway
New York, NY 10036

Cable Vision
Titsch Publishing, Inc.
1130 Delaware Plaza
P.O. Box 4305
Denver, CO 80204

Multi-Channel News
Fairchild Publications, Inc.
P.O. Box 18248
Denver, CO 80218

Television and Radio Age
666 Fifth Avenue
New York, NY 10019

Variety
154 West 46 Street
New York, NY 10036

Public Relations

O'Dwyers Directory of Public Relations Firms
J.R. O'Dwyer and Co., Inc.
271 Madison Avenue
New York, NY 10010

Public Relations News
127 East 80 Street
New York, NY 10021

ORGANIZATIONS FOR MORE INFORMATION ——

American Federation of Television and Radio Artists
1350 Sixth Avenue
New York, NY 10019

American Women in Radio and Television, Inc.
1321 Connecticut Avenue N.W.
Washington, DC 20036

Association of Motion Picture and Television Producers
8480 Beverly Road
Los Angeles, CA 90048

The Cable Television Information Center
1500 North Beauregard Street
Suite 205
Alexandria, VA 22311

National Association of Broadcasters
1771 N. Street N.W.
Washington, DC 20036

National Association of Educational Broadcasters
PACT OFFICE
1346 Connecticut Avenue N.W.
Washington, DC 20036

The National Cable Television Association
1724 Massachusetts Avenue N.W.
Washington, DC 20036

The National Federation of Local Cable Programmers
906 Pennsylvania Avenue S.E.
Washington, DC 20003

National Federation of Press Women, Inc.
Box 99
Blue Springs, MO 64015

Public Relations Society of America, Inc.
845 Third Avenue
New York, NY 10022

Radio-Television News Directors Association
1735 De Sales Street N.W.
Washington, DC 20036

Women in Cable
2033 M. Street N.W.
Suite 703
Washington, DC 20036

5

REAL ESTATE
What's Hot, What's Not

What do Zeckendorf, Helmsley, and Trump all have in common? You guessed it. They have all amassed fortunes in real estate. Why is real estate so hot? Real estate investments have consistently out-performed all other investments combined.

Real estate is an industry that offers opportunity to anyone with imagination, lots of energy, and even a limited amount of cash; financing is always available and desirable. (More on this later.) Thousands of energetic people are making money faster, and in greater amounts than they ever imagined possible. You too could travel this road to self-made wealth.

While there are other kinds of land and property investments, we will explore fast-track careers in residential, commercial, and industrial real estate sales and investments.

THE BROKER

Two thirds of all real estate transactions are arranged by brokers. Nine out of ten homes are sold by brokers and virtually all commercial and industrial properties are sold by brokers. While it is possible to sell one's property without utilizing the professional services of a broker, most people who try to do it fail. Why? When you attempt to sell your property on your own, you are competing with well-established, well-respected real estate agencies and their highly trained, highly motivated and carefully organized marketing and sales force. Also, the broker's reputation and expertise may produce a qualified buyer faster.

The broker earns his/her fee on commission by:

- Qualifying a potential buyer—can he or she afford it? Is he or she likely to get financing? Is he or she a serious buyer, or just a looker?
- Pricing the property at fair market value.
- Marketing the property to sell at fair market value in a reasonable amount of time.
- Acting as a third party in negotiating and knowing effective negotiating techniques.
- Offering expert advice on financing.
- Anticipating and knowing how to avoid legal tangles.

Overall, the real estate broker provides a marketplace where both seller and buyer can meet. While the broker actually has the interests of the owner/seller, the buyer and him or herself at heart, the broker always represents the seller. Upon completion of the sale, the salesperson's fee or commission is paid for by the seller.

National Association of Realtors (NAR)

Ethics, good faith, and loyalty play an important role in the broker/seller and the broker/buyer relationship. Most real estate brokers are professionals who subscribe to a strict code of ethics set forth by the National Association of Realtors. Formed in 1908, the NAR is a not-for-profit organization that has done more to promote professionalism and good will in the real estate business than any other single effort. It is only after agreeing to adhere to these by-laws that a broker may use the term "Realtor," which is a registered trademark of the National Association of Realtors.

LISTINGS

A listing is the contract between the owner and the broker. The listing contract spells out under what terms a sale may be negotiated by the broker; the duration of the contract and the compensation or commission arrangement between the seller and the broker.

There are several kinds of listings:

Exclusive Agency Listing: The broker is assured that he or she will have the exclusive or sole right for a given period of time to negotiate the sale of the property. In return, the broker will usually promote or advertise the property in an effort to sell it. While this arrangement assures the broker that no other broker will earn a commission on the sale of the property, it leaves the door open for the seller to procure a buyer through his or her own efforts. In that case no commission is earned.

Exclusive Right To Sell Listing: Under a written agreement, the broker earns a commission on the sale of the property even if the owner sells the property. If the owner has been negotiating with several prospects before giving the listing to the broker, the owner can protect the right to sell the property to any one of these interested persons by submitting a list of their names to the broker.

Open Listing: This gives the broker the right to act as agent for the seller, but reserves the right of the seller to employ other brokers. Or the owner may sell the property directly, without incurring a broker's fee.

Multiple Listing (MLS):   The property is listed in a centralized data bank of "for sale" properties. A multiple listing is actually an exclusive right-to-sell listing in which the broker is granted authority to make the property known to other brokers. A multiple listing arrangement is advantageous to the owner/seller in that the property gets wider exposure, which tends to mean a higher price and a shorter selling time. MLS refers to the system that centralizes these listings in an effort to share this information. Computer access helps evaluate and compare selling prices of similar properties. The broker pays a small fee for this service.

HOW DO I BEGIN?

There are opportunities in real estate at all levels. You may choose to sell real estate or you may choose to buy *and* sell real estate. In either case, it is necessary to learn about the industry through coursework, training programs, or on the job. Start small; your first few deals will show you the "ins and outs" of real estate negotiation, contracts, and closing. Keep in mind that those people you know who have made successful real estate purchases all started with small properties. The big property owners have usually spent years developing their investments, acquiring larger properties and weeding out the least successful among them.

The License

First, in every state, real estate salespeople must be licensed to sell real property. More specifically, the salesperson must be licensed by the state in which the property is located. In other words, a New Jersey salesperson could not sell property on Connecticut unless he or she was licensed in Connecticut. A Connecticut salesperson could not sell property in Texas, and so on.

To prepare for the sales agent licensing exam, a candidate might take real estate courses offered at the local community college or adult education center, or through a correspondence course. Each state maintains its own authority over exam content, and real estate law, contracts, and other basic concepts are covered. To learn what specific requirements you must meet in order to be eligible to take the exam, you should contact your State Real Estate Commission or your local Board of Realtors.

Learn the Fundamentals

As a real estate salesperson, you will want to become an expert in prospecting, sales psychology, negotiating, real estate law, telephone techniques, financing methods, and closing. Furthermore, if you are specializing—and you should—you will need to be knowledgeable in your area of specialty (i.e., residential, commercial, or industrial). Let's take a closer look.

Each state offers two kinds of real estate licenses: sales agent's license and a broker's license. The two terms are often used interchangeable by an unknowing public but there are distinct differences. The salesperson is licensed to work under the sponsorship and supervision of the broker. The majority of salespersons who show real estate and seek listings are sales agents. Most brokers are self-employed and are busy managing their offices. But it is only the broker who may act as the agent, or enter into a contract to buy, sell or lease property. In most states several years experience and more extensive real estate knowledge are required before a salesperson may sit for the broker's exam.

Education

While a college degree is desirable for someone who wants to sell residential property, it is hardly essential. Good people skills, endless energy and drive are good substitutes. But real estate brokers look for a college degree and even advanced degrees when choosing someone to sell commercial or industrial properties. As we will discuss later in this chapter, commercial and/or industrial sales investing in a sophisticated business requiring more technical knowledge and sophisticated know-how.

Prospecting: How does a real estate agent get in touch with interested buyers? First, the salesperson should be associated with a busy and well respected real estate office; one who advertises listings and whose reputation could bring in potential buyers. Second, one fast-track realtor told us of nine important words every real estate salesperson should live by. "Talk to people, Talk to people, Talk to people." Sound like hype? She assured us it is the single most effective way of finding prospects. And last, ask for referrals—certainly a satisfied customer is your best promotion.

Sales Psychology: Selling real estate requires sales ability and know-how. The same sales techniques and strategies that are effective in other kinds of sophisticated selling are effective in real estate sales too. Some of the most successful and innovative real estate offices offer continual in-house training to their staff.

Real Estate Law: It is necessary for all real estate salespeople to be familiar with the state real estate law as it might effect them or their prospective buyer. There may be local ordinances or zoning restrictions that an agent should be familiar with. The more information the salesperson has at hand, the easier the sale will be.

Telephone Techniques: While showing property requires person-to-person contact, a large part of the salesperson's business is conducted on the telephone. The real estate salesperson must not only conduct routine business on the phone—making appointments, for example—but must be able to interest prospective customers and bring them to the next step of a sale.

It should also be known that while selling is a large part of a salesperson's function, getting listings—the right to sell real property—is also an important function and this is done principally as cold canvassing by telephone. The agent who gets the listing is assured of a percentage of the commission even if someone else actually makes the sale. The commission from a listing may be as much as 10 percent of the earned commission. Updating listings is all done by telephone. Developing a good telephone manner is essential to success in real estate sales.

Financing Methods: Financing plays a major role in almost all real estate purchases. It is important that the agent be aware of and knowledgeable about the kinds of financing available in order to assist the client or potential buyer in obtaining it. (On the positive side, note that 85 percent of all first-time mortgage applications are approved.)

Closing: Specifically, the formal process by which the title of real property passes from seller to buyer. In some parts of the country, this process is called "settlement." If you have been successful in bringing the seller and the buyer together; if the buyer has secured financing as needed and all partners are prepared to close, closing should go smoothly. It is at this point that your effort as sales agent is rewarded. It is only when the deal closes that the broker earns the commission. (There may be some conditions under which the broker is entitled to a fee even though the deal doesn't close.)

RESIDENTIAL REAL ESTATE

Residential sales represents the largest area of sales activity in the industry. Open your newspaper to the real estate pages and you will see page after page of homes and properties "For Sale." If it's springtime, you can expect to read through twice as many advertisements. Residential real estate *is* a seasonal business. Spring and fall are the busiest times of the year for both buying and selling. Prices are usually higher, there are more buyers, and consequently more sales.

Who's Buying?

- *The rich*—sales of larger, more expensive homes are only slightly affected by housing "ups" and "downs."

- *The fast-tracking American dream is alive and well with the fast-tracking baby-boom generation.* These families are buying a smaller "starter" home and not moving up as quickly, but they *are* in the housing market. The condominium and the cooperative housing markets do well with this group because they provide equity and an alternative to expensive single-family home ownership.

- *The "average" American family*—husband, wife, 2.3 kids, and pets are still the largest group of househunters in the nation. In order to get into the housing market, they may be settling for less and using more of their income to do so, but they are still buying.

- *The empty nesters or the more mature.* After the children are gone from the house (usually with homes and families of their own), the parents don't require as much space or don't want to hassle with the upkeep and maintenance of larger homes. They seek the security of ownership and often look towards condominium or retirement villages.

Who's Selling?

People choose to sell their property for any number of reasons including:

- *Relocation, promotion, job change.*   It is important for a buyer to know the circumstances of the relocation. Many companies will buy the homes of their relocating executives outright and not have the *need* to sell the property that an individual would, making it less likely that the home will be a "bargain."

- *Upgrading.*   In our upwardly mobile society, an increase in income may mean the desire for a larger home or one in a more prestigious area.

- *Distress sale.*   Often the house must be sold according to the terms of divorce or other settlement. Some property owners find themselves financially over-extended and must sell in order to raise cash.

- *Repossession.*   The bank reclaims the house for failure of the owner to meet financial obligation. Then the bank sells the house, sometimes by auction.

- *Executors and administrator sale.*   (Also known as estate sales.) Either the family of a deceased owner decides to sell the property in order to settle the estate or, if no will is left, the public administrator may sell the property in order to have liquid assets to divide among any heirs when the estate is settled.

COMPENSATION AND EARNINGS OVERVIEW

Real estate salespeople are compensated on a commission basis. It is fair to say that the neophyte salesperson needs five to six months headway before seeing any commissions. And since most brokers do not pay salary, it would be wise to consider this in your financial plans.

The agreed-upon commission rate between broker and sales agent is negotiable. A 50/50 or 60/40 split is usual. If, for example, a house or property sells for $200,000, the seller is charged 5 percent or $10,000 at an agreed-upon commission rate. Some houses sell for more, some for less. The active sales agent could earn a handsome living by selling residential real estate. Lewis Kay, owner of L.B. Kay Associates, Ltd., one of the largest residential sales organizations in New York City, tells us a good salesperson with three years of experience could earn anywhere from $100,000 to $200,000 in commissions a year. Clearly then, a broker who operates a successful real estate office, employing several successful agents, is on a fast-track to earning big bucks.

COMMERCIAL AND INDUSTRIAL REAL ESTATE

The commercial and industrial real estate marketplace is big business. It takes big bucks, business sophistication, and investment savvy to profit in this end of the real estate business. But if you succeed, profit you will.

As we wrote this section on commercial and industrial real estate, our first inclination was to discuss commercial and industrial real estate investing and sales simultaneously; and while our research uncovered many similarities, the differences were so broad-based that we determined a clear picture could only be drawn by outlining them separately.

What Is Commercial Real Estate?

Commercial real estate relates to office space and buildings, apartment buildings, store properties, shopping centers, theatres, hotels and motels, loft buildings, garages, and vacant commercial sites. Most commercial properties are rental or income-producing properties, although some are bought and sold for (capital) profit alone.

While location is an important feature in buying, selling, and leasing residential property, it is an essential qualifying factor in commercial investments. Consideration for profitability must also be given to how easily accessibility the property is by car and public transportation; adequate parking facilities; availability of labor pool; and proximity of hotels, motels, and restaurants. Airport access is becoming increasingly important, as well. Further considerations in developing commercial property are population size, income level, and accessibility to residential areas. It is clear to see how residential land use would have an impact on commercial property value.

What Is Industrial Real Estate?

Industrial real estate refers to factories, warehouses, utilities, and mines. Industrial real estate tends to be a slow-moving commodity, and the more specialized the facility, the less rapidly it will turn over. Large industrial properties are usually located near urban areas because of their dependence on an adequate labor supply, availability of utilities such as water and central sewers, access to raw material needed in manufacturing, and a marketplace for the finished product. Proximity and access to a freeway or interstate highway is important. Because moving industrial equipment and inventory is expensive and because of loss of services or interruption of business, during a move, an industrial facility tends to remain at one location for an extended time. This means the initial choice of location is most important.

A single industrial park or district might occupy several hundred acres in a large metropolitan area. We were pleased to find that an environmental impact statement is required by the government when an industrial park or district is planned. Finally, the cost or value of a site intended for industrial purposes must be in line with its profit potential.

RESIDENTIAL SALES/INVESTING VS. COMMERCIAL INDUSTRIAL DEALS

Each specialty—residential, commercial, or industrial real estate sales and/or investing—requires knowledge of that particular type of property and clientele.

Selling, leasing, or investing in residential property requires a knowledge of the neighborhood, its schools and other facilities, residential real estate laws, local ordinances (i.e., no street parking after 2 AM, fence heights), and rather simple financing procedures. After twenty hours of classroom study leading to a real estate license, some sales ability and persistence, a sharp salesperson or savvy investor could earn $100,000 or more dealing in residential real estate.

Selling, leasing, or investing in commercial properties requires detailed knowledge of leasing practices, business trends, population shifts, and location needs. Most commercial properties are rental or income-producing properties. They are attractive for that reason or because they qualify the investor or purchaser for tax write-offs.

Selling, leasing, or investing in industrial properties requires detailed and technical knowledge of industry and manufacturing needs, zoning laws, and a rather sophisticated overview of the financing marketplace in order to provide custom and creative financing arrangements. Indeed, the promise of great financial rewards exists but there is a great deal of risk involved as well. The risk to reward ratio is highest in industrial real estate.

How Are They the Same?

Whether residential, commercial, or industrial property, the purchasers desire is to minimize the amount of capital invested in the property. Leverage!

Considerable effort and attention are needed to maximize

the rate of return on any real estate investment. Income property and property management go hand in hand (no matter if the property is residential, commercial, or industrial). Either you are going to manage the property yourself (we hope you are too busy buying up other properties) or you will need to hire a professional—a property manager. The function of a property manager is to oversee the daily routine and advise you of conditions that could affect your investment.

Small or large deal? Residential, commercial, or industrial? No matter. The property must produce a profit in line with the financial risk. If it doesn't, reorganize or resell.

COMMERCIAL AND/OR INDUSTRIAL BROKER —

A person or company is less likely to purchase commercial or industrial real estate directly from a principal owner. The deals are often complicated and require professional assistance. In many deals, the broker is as likely to represent the purchaser or tenant as the owner.

The basic underlying principles of real estate brokerage still prevail, but the commercial and/or industrial salesperson must also have technical understanding of industry's requirement for space. Because there is no multiple-listing service for commercial and industrial properties, there tends to be a high degree of cooperation, referrals, and joint effort among brokers with these specialties. Further, more effort over a longer period of time is usual before a formal contract is signed. Sometimes the commercial and/or industrial brokers will be called upon to come up with a package deal—arrange for a site, construction, lease or sale, financing, and property management.

Income usually increases as an agent gains experience. Individual ability, economic conditions, and the type and location of property also affect earnings.

All in all, the commercial and/or industrial broker needs

to be well-educated (street smarts count as well as classroom accomplishment), sophisticated, eager, and persistent.

EMPLOYMENT OUTLOOK

Selling real estate requires good sales acumen. You need good health and a high energy level, because the fast-track real estate salesperson is actively previewing and showing property throughout an extended working day. Long hours and evening and weekend showings are characteristic of real estate sales. As in all business situations, a good sense of humor is helpful, particularly when dealing with the public. A gentle aggressiveness, coupled with a sincere understanding that the seller may be sentimental about the home being sold and the buyer may be taking on the biggest investment of his or her life may help to close the deal. Being able to schedule efficiently will give a salesperson more time to get listings, to preview and show houses and/or property, and to sell. Overall, those successful brokers/agents who we spoke with told us that providing service, knowledge of the community, and the knowhow to obtain financing that will expedite a deal are all part of successful selling and important ingredients of their $100,000 plus incomes.

INVESTING IN REAL ESTATE

Real estate has proven to be a stable and lasting investment that has weathered many economic ups and downs. And it is worth repeating that real estate has outperformed all other investment vehicles combined. Moreover, real estate has enduring, permanent value.

Investing in real estate *is* a means of acquiring wealth. And most great fortunes, some lesser fortunes, and the guy next door driving that brand new BMW have all invested in real estate.

One needn't have lots of money to make money in real estate. In fact, real property can be bought with little or in some cases no money down. (Later we have included a discussion of financing and leverage.) First-time investors should gauge the cost of the property they acquire in relation to their financial position. In other words, if you have limited resources, start small. Invest in a multi-family dwelling, a small apartment building, or a small shopping strip. If you are particularly handy, buying a "handyman's special," a property that sells for relatively little because it needs considerable restoration or repair, might be an avenue to explore.

Ideally, the rent roll should be greater than the cost of maintenance. At the very least, the promise of an increase in the value of the property should be present. Building equity and using leverage in order to purchase larger properties; or selling at a profit and reinvesting, all represent excellent investment strategies. Clearly the sign of a good investment is profit.

Profile

Alan Ginsberg, 36
The Ginsberg Organization, Inc., New York, NY

Alan Ginsberg had ambition even as a kid, growing up on the streets of Brooklyn, New York. As an enterprising college student who wanted to travel, he set up a travel service for students. Not only did he finance his education from the resources of the Student International Travel Services, but he traveled all over the world. Out of college, he went to work for a large corporation. Even though he admits that he wanted to leave after one month he says, "I didn't want to look like a quitter" and so he stayed on for one year.

A burning desire to get rich brought Ginsberg into the real estate industry. "Real estate always seemed to me to be a business where one could get rich" he says. Ginsberg began as an agent leasing office space. He learned the business by trial and error, working for someone else. Soon he felt the only way he could become financially independent was to go into business for himself.

Enter The Ginsberg Organization, an organization dedicated to aiding the corporate community in a business area they don't really understand. The Ginsberg Organization created a management tool, ANALEASE, which analyzes the overt and covert costs of a lease to the tenant. While most real estate brokers represent the landlord, The Ginsberg Organization was established specifically to assist businesses in dealing with landlords. His dream is eventually to respond to all of the corporation's needs when it comes to purchasing equipment, finding office space, negotiating leases, and all other financial aspects of the deal—all under one roof. Kind of a one-stop shop. Ultimately, what Ginsberg did was identify a need (or a void) and he built a business around this vision.

We asked Ginsberg, "How important is education?" He replied, "My feeling is that education is very important. But for me, the greatest education was people education. Some people call it street smarts. That gives me instincts. The instincts I use in business make the difference between winning and losing. A formal education gives you discipline plus good knowledge. Street smarts gives you common sense instinct."

On his success, Ginsberg says, "I took the risk. I took my money which I earned over the years and I put it on the line. As a result, I did very well, and financially, I became very successful—that is certainly a benefit. The other benefit is that it is nice for me to come here, open the door and see my name on it. It is nice to know that it is my business, and my future is mine. I have peace of mind. I feel good when I wake up and say hey, I built this baby and it is working out!"

Deciding What to Buy

It is important before you invest to define your investment objectives. Begin your search by gathering all the information you can as to what properties are being offered for sale. A local real estate broker can provide a wealth of information about what is currently available and at competitive prices. Cruising potential areas, reading the classified section of the newspaper, and word of mouth may also keep you abreast of property or buildings for sale. Remember though, the best deals are not likely to be the most advertised.

When you think you have located potential investment property, personally inspect it. If a property or building appears to meet your investment criteria, a closer evaluation is in order. This evaluation might include an inspection of available records, (i.e., gas and electric bills, income receipts), analyses of financial statements, possible financing methods, and a projection of potential income. You will want to consider location, trends, and possible shifts in the population and physical conditions *as well as income potential.*

The following is a list of some investment possibilities for the beginner.

- Single family houses to rent or to fix up and resell.

- Multifamily dwellings—possibly two to six families. As an advantage you may consider living in one of the units.

- Small apartment buildings—under ten units.

- Commercial property, small shopping centers or shopping strips.

- A condominium apartment—to rent. Be sure to check the by-laws for any restrictions that might apply.

The amount of cash and mortgaging power or leverage you have, the amount of time and effort you want to devote, and what is available and at what price will all be determining factors in what you decide to buy.

What about Financing?

How much cash is needed? Generally speaking, 20 percent of the purchase price.

It is easier to finance other real estate investments after you have acquired your first. With your first investment and subsequent investments you build equity, the value the investor/owner has in a piece of property minus its mortgage. For example, if the market value of a house or property is $100,000 and the owner owes the mortgage lender $60,000, the owner has accrued $40,000 in equity. Simply put, a lender will now loan you up to the amount of equity you have accrued, or in this case up to $40,000. What is significant about this is that you now have use of the capital represented by the equity build-up in your home or property and can use that money to invest further in order to enhance your wealth.

In current real estate jargon this is called *leverage*, OPM (other people's money), or pyramiding. In fact, it is this set of circumstances—the ability to acquire real estate with a large percentage of borrowed money—that makes real estate such an attractive investment. The higher the leverage, the greater the potential for profit. In other words, $20,000 could control a $100,000 investment, $200,000 could control a $1,000,000 investment. The greater the amount of borrowed money compared to the equity cash, the greater the leverage. Further, the greater the equity or leverage, the more property the investor can buy. Building equity and using leverage to buy larger and more expensive property is an excellent investment strategy. The potential for financial wealth by investing in real estate is great because the leverage obtained through borrowing money is great.

Financial Terms ————————————————————————

It is not unusual for one lender to offer five, six, or more different mortgage instruments, at interest rates that might range over three full percentage points. If you are borrowing $80,000 over years, the difference of just one-half of percentage point could mean thousands of dollars over the course of the loan. So shop around for the best mortgage terms (interest rate and cash outlay) to suit your particular needs. There are many kinds of financing available. Talk with several mortgage lenders and your accountant before making a commitment.

SETTING UP A BUSINESS (ORGANIZATION) ————

This chapter on fast-track real estate careers would be incomplete without a discussion of income tax advantages. Because tax laws are changing, we will not cite specific tax advantages. Suffice it to say, that real estate is the best tax shelter we know of.

Further, by organizing your real estate purchases in a business framework, you may take advantage of still more tax benefits and incentives. The form of business organization you choose will effect your ability to control decision making power, your liability and any tax advantages derived from your real estate investments. Various forms of business organizations include sole proprietorship, partnership, corporation, subchapter S corporation, and real estate syndicate.

Because of the "coming of age" and increased income of the baby boom generation, the demand for residential and investment real estate will increase over the next decade. Continued inflation will play a role in keeping real estate the number one investment vehicle.

There are indeed fast-track careers in the real estate industry. Whether you sell real estate or invest in real estate, the promise of big bucks is clearly there.

GLOSSARY

Adjustable Interest Rate:
A fluctuating interest rate that can go up or down, depending on the index.

Agent:
A person who is authorized to represent or act on behalf of another.

Amortization:
The liquidation of a financial obligation using regular equal payments on an installment basis.

Broker:
An agent licensed by the state, who for a fee negotiates the sale or lease of real property for another.

Closing:
In the sale of real estate it is the final moment when all documents are executed and recorded and the sale is complete.

Commission:
The fee earned by a broker for his services. Usually a percentage of the selling price, or of the rent in the case of a lease.

Conventional Mortgage:
See "fixed-rate."

Creative Financing:
Alternative financing methods, for example, seller-assisted financing.

Equity:
The value that an owner has in property over and above the liens against it.

Exclusive Agency:
A real estate broker who has the sole right to sell a property within a specified period of time.

Exclusive Right to Sell:
A written contract between agent and owner where the agent has the right to collect a commission if the property is sold by anyone during the term of the agreement.

Federal National Mortgage Association (FNMA):
A government sponsored, privately owned corporation that supplements private mortgage market operations. Also known as Fannie Mae.

Fixed Rate or Conventional Mortgage:
A loan at one stated interest rate over the entire term of the mortgage.

General Partnership:
The operating or managing partner in a limited partnership.

Leverage:
The use of a small amount of value to control a much larger amount of value.

Liability:
A term covering all types of debts and obligations.

Lien:
An encumbrance against real property for money, as in taxes, mortgages, judgments.

Limited Partner:
The silent partner in a general partnership. The limited partner is exempt by law from liability in excess of their contribution. Also, the limited partner cannot participate in management.

Listing:
A contract between owner and broker to sell the owner's property.

Mortgage:
A pledge of real property as security for a deal or obligation.

Mortgage Banker:
Individual who makes mortgage loans with the expectation of reselling them to an institutional lender.

Mortgage Broker:
A person who, for a fee, brings together a borrower with a lender.

Multiple Listings (MLS):
A computerized data bank of all subscribing brokers and their listings.

National Association of Realtors (NAR):
Formed in 1908, a not-for-profit organization that sets professional guidelines for the industry.

Negative Amortization:
When the allocation of the payment between principle and interest is changed, the principle balance being increased periodically by the addition of the unpaid interest.

Open Listing:
Gives the broker the right to sell but reserves the right of the seller to employ other brokers.

Promissory Note:
A statement acknowledging a debt and the terms under which it is to be repaid, signed by the borrower.

Realtor:
A registered trademark of the National Association of Realtors denoting a licensed real estate broker who is a member of a local board affiliated with the NAR.

Sole Proprietorship:
A form of business ownership whereby one individual controls and manages the business activity.

Sub Chapter S Corporation:
A form of business organization with favorable tax benefits if you qualify.

Syndicate:
A combination of individuals who invest in a particular venture which otherwise would be too large for each individual.

Veteran's Administration (VA):
The VA is a federal agency which offers a loan guarantee program to qualified veterans, usually at a low interest rate. Sometimes referred to as GI loans.

WHAT YOU SHOULD BE READING

The Home Buying Veteran
VA Pamphlet 26-6
Free—Call your local Veteran's Administration Office

The Intelligent Investor's Guide to Real Estate
William Walters, et al.
John Wiley & Sons Inc.: New York, NY

The Real Estate Almanac
Robert D. Allen and Thomas E. Wolfe
John Wiley & Sons Inc.: New York, NY

Real Estate Today
107 Washington Avenue
P.O. Box 122
Albany, NY 12260

The Smart Investor's Guide to Real Estate
Robert Brus
Crown Publishers, Inc.: New York, NY

ORGANIZATIONS FOR MORE INFORMATION ——

American Society of Real Estate Counselors
430 North Michigan Avenue
Chicago, IL 60611
312-440-8000

National Association of Realtors
430 North Michigan Avenue
Chicago, IL 60611
312-329-8292

The National Association of Real Estate Brokers
5501 Eighth Street N.W. Suite 202
Washington, DC 20011
202-829-8500

National Institute of Realtors
Department of Education
155 East Superior Street
Chicago, IL 60611

U.S. Department of Housing and Urban Development (HUD)
451 8th Street S.W.
Washington, D.C. 20410

Women's Council of Realtors
430 North Michigan Avenue
Chicago, IL 60611
312-440-8000

6

EXECUTIVE SEARCH
Headhunting as a Career

There was a time when the executive recruiter was the person behind the palm in a hotel lobby. Today there is nothing sneaky, deceptive or mysterious about executive recruiting. It is simply another business. It serves clients who want a third party to go out and ethically find somebody in the marketplace to fit a certain job.

—Executive Search Firm Owner
Houston, Texas

It is a professional jungle out there and the big-game hunters are the executive search consultants. Maybe that's why the job title is frequently interchanged with terms like headhunter, corporate pirate, and body snatcher. Executive search consultants hate these terms and many are working extremely hard to improve and upgrade the image of the industry. The rampant careerism of the eighties has helped to give new respectability to this once frowned on profession and it is suddenly very "in." Almost everyone finds it an ego-building experience to receive a recruitment call from a search consultant.

Executive search firms are currently used by over 90 percent of *Fortune* 500 corporations and by many small-to-medium-sized organizations. Gilbert Dwyer and Company of

New York Associates comments, "Executive Search is a rapidly growing business. More and more areas of human endeavor are discovering search and using it. For example, university management is relatively new in using executive search as are health care institutions. Even government, which may be the last bastion, has begun using professional recruiters. The market for executive search appears to be expanding constantly, and I have no reason to think that it will stop."

The growing popularity of search firms is a by-product of the overwhelming interest in careers by the baby boom set. Today, there are fast-trackers in corporations using search firms to staff their organizations and there are fast-trackers on the opposite side hoping to have a search firm contact them with a dream opportunity.

Recruitment as a profession first began when there was a different work ethic in the labor market—when job hopping was frowned upon. Hiring people away from a company was difficult, employees were nervous about being contacted by a recruiter. Nowadays, a call from a recruiter may represent career achievement; in fact, job changes are regarded with less suspicion than previously, particularly for the recognized fast-tracker. People are changing jobs more frequently, as well as earlier in their careers, to broaden their experience base. Individuals have a new attitude toward their own welfare; and loyalty to a company rarely gets in the way of the executive recruiter's quest.

WHAT IS IT ALL ABOUT?

The market area for employment recruiting usually involves people who are currently employed. A corporation will engage a search firm to locate a qualified candidate for a specific management position. Currently, there are approximately 2000 recognized executive search firms and scores and scores more of individual consultants.

A search firm works for the client company, *not* the job hunter. Recruiters report that 99 percent of the people they contact during the search are employed and the majority are happily employed; however, almost all listen to what the recruiter has to offer. Being contacted by a search consultant is welcomed by most executives because it means they have visibility within their field and are recognized for their work.

Business today operates on the star system. Whether a company is grossing $1 billion or $1 million, they want a miracle worker to keep profits flowing. A company is willing to pay a search consultant handsomely to find the superstars they need to boost profits. Recruiting firms can make life considerably easier for the corporation. They know who's who in the industry, what talents the individual has and whether he or she is emotionally and philosophically right for the company seeking an executive.

Executive search professionals have access to corporate executives who would be unreachable to most individual organizations. Bear in mind, the majority of the prospective candidates who are contacted and lured by the recruiters, are *not* presently job hunting.

In addition to a search firm's ability to scout out specific talent, the recruiter offers third party objectivity. Not only can the firm separate itself from the internal politics of the client organization, but it frequently forces management to face facts. Sometimes the corporate messiah envisioned by the client is neither a realistic nor appropriate ideal. Because of a search firm's intensive involvement with a client's inner workings, its staff can often express (with a degree of authority) what management teams and executive boards cannot say to each other, but would like to. In short, a search firm does not have the emotional involvement of an internal hiring committee. (It also serves as a convenient scapegoat if the newly appointed executive doesn't work out.)

Confidentiality is a key issue. Competitors and internal staff cannot (and should not) always know what management plans are in the works. An executive being replaced may not even know the search is on.

IS THIS FIELD FOR ME?

It may be . . . if you are hardworking, possess a keen intuitive people sense and are aware of your own manipulative selling skills. Since confidentiality and discretion are critical components, gossip lovers should avoid this field at all costs. A college degree is an unwritten, but understood prerequisite.

"Executive Search is a selling business. You've got to be aggressive, persistent, personable, and bright. It is a highly sophisticated consulting business in which you are selling your judgment and your experience to a client who is essentially all of these same things and who has a relatively high place in the organization," reports Gilbert Dwyer. In our discussions with recruiters, we found that many felt that a wide variety of client activity enhances their work. One recruiter noted, "In the course of one year, you might find yourself in finance, medicine, personnel, or research management. Clients might range from those in the oil business to the insurance business. This diversity is one of the joys of recruiting and allows it to be distinguished from other corporate work."

One suggested route for entering the field is to come in as a "backroom recruiter"—that is an individual who does research and heavy telephone solicitation. Of course, since much of the excitement of recruitment is in interacting with senior management and securing and directing the search, this route is relatively unglamorous. Another professional advocated the idea of building a mini-career first that could translate easily into executive search. This means you should develop a corporate posture and build up credibility in an industry so you can do recruitment in a specialized area.

Profile

Robin Rube, 34
Robin A. Rube Associates, New York, NY

Robin Rube is quickly establishing herself as a successful consultant in the area of attorney search. Her contingency firm, Robin A. Rube Associates, was founded in 1982 after Rube had worked for some time at a very large executive search firm. Prior to that, after graduating from law school in 1978 she was a prosecutor in the Family Court of Manhattan. She is sole principal, and business is going very well.

"I truly believe that this business was made for me. You have to be a matchmaker at heart and you really have to have a sense of people." Rube, who is married, says she wants to have it all . . . career and family too. Her own business, and particularly the search business, may allow her to fulfill these dreams.

Rube's advice to aspirants to careers in this area is to get into an established search firm and watch someone who has been doing it for a while. "To get going takes a long time. It takes a lot of experience, unending patience, and persistence, numerous breakfasts, lunches, and dinners, but mostly honesty and, subsequently, credibility." Rube says that to consider yourself successful in the search business, an individual should be making a six-figure income.

"Being a search consultant is equivalent to a balancing act. There are a lot of people who do what I do and do it differently. I believe in helping a person to choose which option is truly the best, however; a good consultant must be aware of the fine line that exists between being informative and being overly aggressive."

Rube and others are finding success early in executive search because the market of talent continues to grow younger. Once grey-haired recruiters searched for grey-haired CEOs. Today, fast-trackers are in vogue and, therefore, fast-tracking recruiters have found an entirely new industry opening its doors to them.

One minor point of caution—executive search conjures up a fairly shoddy image for many job hunters and employers. Ignoring this "sleaze factor" is important to ensure your success. This unfortunate perception is due to ambitious recruiters who utilize techniques to locate prime executives that are legal, but are considered unscrupulous by many.

Can I Make Money?

Absolutely!!! According to *Money* magazine (December 1986), executive search rookies earn an average of $70,000 annually, while veterans top in at $150,000 per year. *Money* cited a vice president at a major New York City firm who earns $300,000. Search consultants normally work on a commission basis and take home up to 40 percent commission on the fee generated by the placement.

Ultimately, when you are an executive recruiter dealing with America's corporate elite, you will find executive search to be an *extremely* lucrative profession. Big money is paid to the search consultant who lures a CEO from one turf to another. Perhaps every bit as important as the income is the glory and respect a recruiter earns for stealing away a corporate messiah. It was Korn/Ferry who put Peter Uberroth into the position of president of the Los Angeles Olympic Organizing Committee. Heidrick and Struggles put John Sculley into the president's seat at Apple Computer. The list is endless. Of course, it takes time, expense, and savvy to play in the executive search big leagues; however, search consultants in the early stages of their careers still stand to do well, especially in a positive economy when the search is on for middle management executives.

New York City once again tops the charts as the recruitment capital. Other popular American cities in this industry include:

Chicago
Denver
Atlanta
Dallas/Houston
Los Angeles

Naturally, the concentration of clients or prospective clients will influence where a search firm is set up. You need to find a relatively sophisticated and economically sound market where people are willing to pay the high fees associated with search firm activity.

The staff of a search firm may be extremely diverse. At one search firm we found two attorneys, three computer technicians with software expertise, one Ph.D. in chemistry, and five people with a background in manufacturing. All of these individuals were taking part in the search process.

New specialty areas at search firms include: finance, real estate, energy, hospitality/leisure, textiles, pharmaceutical manufacturing, and hospital administration. If you have a connection with any one of these fields, you may already have a good head start on a search career!

THE SEARCH SYSTEM

Executive search firms typically handle searches for personnel at or above the $60,000 salary level. A few firms may go as low as $30,000-a-year executives, and of course the major search firms go far beyond the $60,000 figure. *U.S. News and World Report* surveyed 202 of the largest U.S. companies with revenues topping 2.9 billion dollars and found that over one-half of the hundred highest paying executives earned over a million dollars in salary compensation packages.

Contingency vs. Retainer Firms ─────────────────

Essentially, the recruitment industry entertains two types of candidates. Employment agencies (which we'll discuss later), are *not* search firms—they focus on an unemployed market. Search firms deal with an *employed* manpower market. The candidates they work with are typically already in a position and the search firm has been hired by the client to locate and lure away the executive best meeting their specifications, rather than work with a pool of available applicants.

Within the field of executive search, the definitions grow finer still. As you learn more and more about this field, you will hear search firms referred to as either contingency or retainer. At the time of this writing there are approximately 1800 contingency firms and approximately 1000 retained firms in the United States. Both types of firms profess to be in the business of executive search (and they are). The big difference is in how the client company pays for the conducted search. A retained firm is paid regardless of whether or not they aid the client in finding an appropriate candidate. So, win or lose, a retained firm has still made money. (Do not confuse a retained firm with a yearly retainer. A retained firm can work on a single search.) A contingency firm is paid if and only if the search has been successful.

The distinction between these two types of search firms has given birth to a discreet prejudice among industry personnel. The retained firms enjoy the advantages of their selective positions and tend to look down on the contingency firms, often passing them off as "poor step-sisters." While the major firms in the industry are retainer paid, it still does not diminish the success that contingency firms have experienced.

When an organization employs a search firm it gives great

consideration to the fee structure; but it rarely makes a difference to the candidate how the search is being paid for. Candidates feel, therefore, that they have little to lose in investigating a recruiting opportunity. A candidate is never obliged to pay a search firm a fee.

Retained firms argue that the only issue at large is confidentiality, as well as the art of the search. Because contingency firms only make money by producing an appropriate candidate, many minimize the search process and spend more time forwarding resumes than playing matchmaker. In the business this may be referred to as a "cattle car approach." This hit-and-miss philosophy is scorned by the retained firms, who argue that an executive's career may be in jeopardy if the employer learns that the individual is in the market for a new position. On the plus side for contingency firms is the fact that over half the business done in executive search is handled by contingency organizations.

Depending on the search firm and the assignment, an executive recruiter's fee is typically 20 percent to 35 percent or roughly one-third of the candidate's first year's compensation package. For the most part, the current magic number is $33\frac{1}{3}$ percent, although industry experts predict it will hit 40 percent by 1990. Retained firms handle searches for positions of $60,000 or above. Most contingency firms take on searches falling in the $35,000 to $75,000 range. This is not a clearly defined rule and there are always exceptions. Executive recruiters who have built a real following and have earned a reputation among corporations as experts in the search field have the luxury of turning down searches that will not generate substantial fees. Those who have reached this relatively exclusive status are *not* newcomers and are admittedly exceptional at what they do.

Companies that work with retainer firms will usually pay one-third of the retainer at the outset of the search (called a "front end retainer"), one third at the end of 30 days and the final third at the conclusion of 60 days. A client also picks up all out-of-pocket expenses incurred by the search firm, which are typically 10 to 20 percent of the fee. As an industry, executive search firms annually bill more than 1.5 billion dollars in search fees.

ANATOMY OF A SEARCH

Let us assume you could observe all the steps of a search from its start through its completion. Here is a synopsis of the activities you might be privy to.

In Stage 1 the client contacts the search firm and a profile of the desired executive is drawn up. In Stage 2 the search is conducted. Eventually, the search firm will produce three to six individuals whose skills and experiences most closely resemble the profile discussed with the client. In Stage 3, the client makes its choice and the search firm then goes about luring the individual away from the current employer. It may sound easy, but it is in fact, an extremely detailed and sometimes lengthy process. Most searches take from three to four months, with much of the work being done in the first month.

A search consultant will spend up to one week or more interviewing the client. An exact job description is crucial to the success of the search. Usually ten or more of the client's key staff members are singled out to meet with the consultant. The consultant will get executive specifics and will study the corporate chemistry. The search firm will evaluate the CEO and his or her existing staff and may even speak with clerical support staff to get an overall flavor of the organization. One recruiter told us he likes to meet with an executive who has recently been promoted. The recruiter likes to find out why the executive has advanced and make his own appraisal. As the recruiter explained, apparently, the client has judged that this individual has the "right stuff," so he likes to see what the employee is all about—what, in the client's eyes, "the right stuff" is.

Once a profile of the desired executive has been drawn and both the client and the search firm are in agreement on the executive's job description, the consultant begins to research the marketplace. The process and procedures may vary depending on whether the firm is a contingency firm or retainer based; however, for the purpose of this overview, we will outline the process in a general way.

The names of respected prospects are solicited through networking. Files are reviewed of all those who have corresponded with the search firm within the last six months, unsolicited resumes are looked over. The firm may run an ad to find a pool of available candidates. In-house directories are vital to a search consultant and many search firms have compiled numerous directories of trade associations. The very large search firms all have computerized data banks and search factors are keyed in, possible candidates are printed out.

At the industry's "Big 6" search firms, thousands of names are reviewed in computerized data files of those individuals with industry visibility. Publications and trade journals are seriously scanned for new stars. Reference books such as Dunn & Bradstreet's *Book of Corporate Management* are checked out. For some searches, cold calling may be done. One excellent source of information for recruiters who are doing cold calling is a company switchboard or the firm's secretarial staff. Recruiters may get biographical data on the pretext of doing an industry survey or compiling a directory of Who's Who in the field.

Once consultants have identified a prospective candidate, they use the tool of the profession . . . the telephone. On a recruitment call, after an introduction, a recruiter explains that a search is being conducted for a key executive. The client is not revealed, but the position is described briefly, with its salary range and geographic locale. A contingency firm may or may not actually meet the candidate. It is possible for the recruiter to arrange an interview with the client after the phone call or after reviewing the individual's resume. Retained firms will *always* meet the candidate. At this meeting, the consultant will judge the chemistry factor of the individual and how he or she might fit into the client organization. The candidate's appearance, polish, and business savvy will be evaluated. His or her management philosophy and professional achievements will be discussed at some length. The consultant will provide further information about the position and reveal the identity of the client.

Depending on the search firm, a real employment opportunity may or may not exist when a recruiter meets a candidate. Some recruiters meet hot candidates simply to determine their marketability. In this industry, candidates are commodities and one is either finding the executive for the opening or peddling the executive to a company. Search firms that are dealing with a client company on an exclusive basis will have a bonafide opening to discuss. The search consultant and the candidate talk specifics and if the prospect looks good the recruiter must be able to sell the candidate on his/her client. This is clearly the time when the candidate has the best possible bargaining power. The consultant will note the individual's "demands" and report them to the client, should the candidate be selected for presentation. Some search firms will go as far as to interview the candidate's spouse, so that any vetoes are weeded out before the client company gets involved. Said one recruiter, "Relocation, more travel, longer hours, a higher degree of stress should be considered by the candidate. I want to air the disadvantages as well as the advantages . . . you want the executive to accept and be happy, not tell you two weeks into the job that it was a mistake."

Finally, the search firm refers several executives for review to the client. This is done on paper and by telephone first and then in-person interviews are set up. During the hiring process a consultant will act as the go-between for client and candidate. A successful match means politicking for money and perks for the candidate while negotiating a fee with the client. It is the search firm that "closes the sale" with the candidate once an offer has been extended by the client company.

Rules of the Search Game

The first snag in the system came about when firms promised never to raid their own clients—that is, not steal executives from an organization with which they had done business. Originally, this was a self-imposed hands-off rule that lasted for a two year period. The rule, however, proved self-defeating, since it meant that as a search firm grew, its hunting grounds for potential executives diminished. The Big 6 firms particularly felt the ruling unfair, since their client companies took advantage of it by hiring the firm at least once every two years to fill low-paying positions and thereby made their companies continue off-limits to the search firm. It meant raids were off indefinitely.

An alternative solution to this problem has been to set a dollar amount of business or a set number of searches a client company does with a search firm, thus ensuring the protection of their executives from a raid. The dollar figure and search number may be determined by client size. Still other organizations keep a search firm on a permanent retainer to keep their management intact.

THE BIG 6

Ad agencies have the Big 10, accounting firms have the Big 8 and search firms have the Big 6. The best and brightest of the search firms are noted as follows:

1. Korn/Ferry International
   1800 Century Park East
   Suite 900
   Los Angeles, CA 90067
   213-879-1834

2. Heidrick & Struggles
   125 South Wacker Drive
   Suite 2800
   Chicago, IL 60606
   312-372-8811

3. Spencer Stuart & Associates
   55 East 52nd Street
   New York, NY 10055
   212-407-0200

4. Russell Reynolds Associates (N.Y.)
   245 Park Avenue
   New York, NY 10167
   212-953-4300

5. Boyden Associates
   260 Madison Avenue
   New York, NY 10016
   212-685-3400

6. Egon Zehnder International
   645 Fifth Avenue
   New York, NY 10022
   212-838-9199

EMPLOYMENT AGENCIES

Depending on whom you talk to, employment agencies and search firms are either close relatives or two species from different planets.

We have chosen to link them in this chapter because

many fast-tracking executive search professionals trace their roots back to the employment business. In both professions, job candidates are marketed to a client organization which is (in almost all cases) paying a hiring fee. The big differences between a search firm and an employment agency are largely:

- Employment agency applicants approach the agency (and are always welcome).
- Employment agencies operate on a higher profile, their openings are more visible (there is heavy recruitment advertising).
- The positions an agency handles generally fall in the $10,000 to $40,000 category.
- Employment agency applicants are generally unemployed, rather than currently employed.

Today, almost all agencies operate on a "fee paid" basis wherein the client company, not the applicant, pays the agency fee. Like the contingency search consultant, the agency counselor/placement manager is paid on commission and receives a fee only if a successful placement is made. While different agencies charge different fees, it is reasonable to assume the fee will generally be 1 percent per thousand of the first year's salary. For example, an $18,000 position commands an 18 percent fee or $3240. From this amount the counselor's portion is roughly 30 to 50 percent.

Getting in . . .

Aspirants to the agency business have only to look in the classified ads under Personnel, Placement, or Sales. There is a high turnover in the industry and openings almost always exist. Before joining an employment agency, visit its offices as a potential applicant. Check out the corporate decor, how you are treated and whether or not you feel comfortable with the level of professionalism. Ask anyone you know in personnel positions which agencies they hire from and who has the best reputation.

Agencies largely look for aggressiveness, motivation, excellent people skills, and above all, sales ability in their staff. As a newcomer you may undergo a corporate training program or you may simply be placed at a desk with a phone and yellow pages. Much of a placement manager's day is spent on the phone marketing to companies. Most agency people tell you the hard part is getting the job orders, that recruiting candidates is easy. New placement managers generally start with a low base or draw versus commission and almost all will tell you the first six months are the hardest. First you must establish yourself with client companies and then you need to build a referral service of applicants from satisfied placements. Is it profitable? Read the following profile and see for yourself.

Profile

Stephanie Shapiro, 31
Career Blazers Agency, Inc., New York, NY

Stephanie Shapiro has been in the placement industry for just 4 short years and in 1986 she earned in excess of $120,000. Shapiro graduated from college with a BA in political science and went on to earn a masters in social work from Columbia University. She chose social work for its diversity and people concentration and spent three years in the field before her experience soured. "I was working for a city hospital where the patients were short stay. I had limited contact with them and I couldn't make any kind of impact or give any help. It was extremely frustrating."

While still employed, Shapiro began networking and researching her possibilities. "I had a friend at Macmillan publishing who sent me to Career Blazers. . . . I knew the score, I was a college grad who couldn't type and there weren't too many jobs out there for me in business. I knocked on doors to become a gal Friday." Career Blazers solution to Shapiro's employment dilemma was to offer her a job in placement. Shapiro started doing secretarial and clerical placements for six months before she transferred into Career Blazers Law Services Division to do paralegal placement. In her first year, Shapiro earned $19,000. "It took me a year to learn the business . . . to get motivated and realize I could make a lot of money at this."

Asked to provide five characteristics of a good placement professional, Shapiro offered, "Assertiveness, intuitiveness, ability to be a self-starter, competitiveness, and malleableness." Although she's never been a paralegal herself, in 1986 Shapiro placed 153 paralegals in the city's top law firms. Her client base consists of fifteen strong, consistent clients and ten sporadic clients. She feels a college degree is essential as is a bit of "life experience." "My clients trust me. I've learned to listen and really hear—from both sides, the client and the applicant. Then you make matches." Shapiro claims that on a scale of 1–10, she is a 10 in competition. "I have to be number one, but I keep preparing myself for a bad year. Realistically, I know you can't keep the production level I'm at every year, so I keep waiting."

Shapiro laughs when you ask her if she puts in 80-hour work weeks. "I'm the luckiest person alive . . . it's basically 9 to 5!" Her work ethic is to work hard and be honest. "I do everything I do in good conscience. You can work hard, be competitive, and still be ethical."

Asked if she loves her job, Shapiro says "love" isn't in her vocabulary for her career. "It's a great job when everything is going wonderfully. This is a job of peaks and valleys. And there are times when everything I touch turns to gold and it's amazing and I can't believe my good fortune. Then there are times when you run into bad periods when things just don't gel. . . . I'm glad I took the risk and changed careers, I still have friends who are in social work and are having problems with it. They're in awe of what I'm earning, I'm in awe of what I'm earning, my father's in awe, my husband's in awe . . . it's crazy!"

GLOSSARY

Applicant:
The job seeker.

Candidate:
An applicant who has been qualified by a search firm as a possible placement for the client opening.

Client:
In executive search and other personnel placement areas, the client is the individual or company paying the fee. It is almost always the employer.

Contingency:
A payment arrangement between client and search firm in which a fee is paid by the client only if a candidate has been found and hired through the search consultant.

Employment Agency:
An operation that deals largely with an unemployed manpower market. The firm brings together employers and applicants, generating successful "matches" between the two parties. Fees may be paid by either the employer or applicant.

Executive Recruiter:
The name given to a search professional who is in the business of seeking an executive to fill an opening listed by the client company. (Slang: headhunter, corporate pirate, body snatcher.)

Placement:
The successful match between client company and candidate.

Retainer:
A payment arrangement between client and search firm in which a fee is paid by the client, regardless of whether or not a suitable candidate has been found.

WHAT YOU SHOULD BE READING

Directory of Executive Consultants
Consultant's News
Templeton Road,
Fitzwilliam, NH 03447

Provides a listing of executive search firms, their specialization and geographic locale. Kennedy & Kennedy of *Consultant's News* also publishes a monthly newsletter for the industry. Information on this publication is available at the address listed or by calling (603) 585-2200.

Executive Employment Guide
The Management Information Service
American Management Association
135 W. 50th St., NY, NY 10020
A listing of 150 search firms and related bibliography.

Executive Musical Chairs
William Wilkinson
Published by Warrinton & Co.,
San Mateo, CA, 1983

How to Answer a Head Hunter's Call: A Complete Guide to Executive Search
Robert H. Perry
Published by AMACOM, NY, 1984

The Prentice-Hall Directory of Executive Search Firms
William Lewis & Carol Milano
Offers a resource of over 1800 executive search firms arranged by field and by location.

Secrets of a Corporate Head Hunter
John Wareham
Published by Atheneum, NY, 1980

ASSOCIATIONS & ORGANIZATIONS

Association of Executive Search Consultants
(formerly Association of Executive Recruitment Consultants)
30 Rockefeller Plaza
New York, NY 10112

The National Employment Association of Personnel Consultants
1432 Duke Street
Alexandria, VA 22314

7

SALES
Where You Make It Happen

70k 1st Year Potential. Seeking a successful sales professional with management potential to enter our fast-track management training program. If you are . . . a proven closer, mostly motivated, success-oriented salesperson looking for a solid career opportunity with a great future, call for confidential interview.

Open to the employment pages of your Sunday paper and scan the help wanted ads. You'll find advertisements for accountants, administrative assistants, bookkeepers, nurses, paralegals, and programmers. Don't stop turning the pages until you have reached the sales category and *then* start reading. You'll find advertisements much like the one above promising a fast-track management and a fast-track to earning big bucks.

It has been said of business that "nothing happens until somebody sells something" and indeed, sales is the lifeblood of our economy. In fact, salespeople are responsible for generating more revenue into our economy than any other single profession. More than six million men and women are employed as sales professionals—and that implies a lot of selling.

WHY CHOOSE SALES?

- Selling is challenging. The harder it is to sell someone the more challenging and creative the sale.
- There are a wide variety of jobs available.
- Sales offers a stable career choice. Career opportunities are unlimited. A good salesperson will always find a job. One sales professional told us she could sell anything. She would need to learn the language related to her product but sell she could!
- Selling offers immediate gratification. No need to wait for a pat on the back from a superior—closing the deal is reward enough.
- The financial rewards of a sales career is what attracts most salespeople. It is not uncommon for top salespeople to earn incomes equivalent to those of top corporate managers.
- Successful salespeople are recognized by upper management. Many key corporate positions are held by men and women who began their careers selling. Combine super salesmanship with common sense and an even temperament and you may ride the fast lane to management.

Is a Sales Career Right for You?

Do you enjoy challenge?
Do you enjoy meeting new people?
Are you a self starter?
Are you a good listener?
Are you goal oriented?
Can you cope with competition?
Can you handle rejection?

If you answered 'Yes' to these questions a sales career might be right for you. Successful salespeople enjoy and thrive on new and unexpected challenges. They love selling and are hungry for money and success (and not necessarily in that order). The successful salesperson is a self starter who is motivated by competition. He or she knows there is a direct relationship between effort and reward and is willing to put in that added effort to succeed.

Sales can be a fast track into management. If you are seeking the challenge and status of being part of a management team, a sales position lays a good foundation. Generally speaking, companies take their best salespeople and promote them into management positions. When companies hire experienced sales staff, they often look for a combination of sales ability and leadership qualities.

Do I Have a Sales Personality?

It takes all kinds of personalities to sell. It helps to be outgoing, but we interviewed salespeople whom we considered introverted. You think you need to be fast talking? We met fast-tracking, slow talkers earning $100,000 plus a year. You do need to be sincere and honest, intelligent, with common sense; self-confident, enthusiastic; persuasive (this can be learned), well-groomed, and ambitious.

We interviewed salespeople whose enthusiasm alone generated interest in their product. One sales manager told us he considered enthusiasm a reasonable substitute for experience. Furthermore, we learned that the art of selling *can* be learned. Companies like IBM and Xerox invest thousands of dollars in sales training programs and seminars because they are effective in developing a professional motivated sales staff.

Belief in yourself and your product are essential to success in sales. Above all, the desire to make money is the driving force behind most successful salespeople. Successful salespeople know that to earn more, they simply have to sell more.

Finally, many different personality characteristics make a salesperson successful and individuals with widely different personalities and backgrounds have "made it" in sales. Why not you?

WHERE THE JOBS ARE AND HOW TO FIND THEM

Sales job opportunities are wherever business is conducted, from small entreprenuerial ventures to large corporations. The right sales opportunity for you may exist right where you are, with your present employer. If you like the company you are working for, talk to the sales manager. Or, you might seek employment outside your company. In either case, plan your strategy and promote yourself.

Often the knowledge and experience you have acquired in your current job could be transferred into a sales career. We interviewed a nurse who transferred her nursing skills into selling pharmaceuticals; a computer programmer who is earning megabucks selling computer software; and a secretary earning more money selling word processing equipment than she ever dreamed possible. The possibilities are endless. Use the expertise you've gained in your working career to create opportunities in sales.

When applying for a sales position, seek out and speak directly to the sales manager. When sending your resume, address it to the sales manager by name. Include a cover letter designed to pique the interest of the sales manager. It should be custom written, polite and to the point. Of course, refer to your enclosed resume and ask for an interview.

Keep informed. Read business and trade publications. *The Wall Street Journal, Business Week, Dun's Review, Fortune* and *Forbes* are filled with product announcements and new business developments. Trade publications often carry employment advertisements and specific information to the trade. Both business and trade publications may give you insight into industry hot spots. Remember, where there is growth, there are jobs. Not only will these publications and others keep you informed about business, they also provide excellent leads.

In today's competitive marketplace you need to react quickly and efficiently to get the best jobs. Keep in mind that an experienced and successful salesperson can always find a job. Good salespeople are in demand in any industry.

Education

Do I need a degree? While a degree might be required if you sell hi-tech communications equipment, or desirable if you sell stocks, for the majority of sales jobs street smarts will suffice. A well-rounded education of some kind is critical, however, for a successful sales career where communication skills lay the foundation for sales success.

What about Training?

All companies offer some kind of sales training. Larger companies like IBM and Xerox provide extensive training programs for their new recruits. Smaller companies, on the other hand, often offer less formal training, usually by a seasoned salesperson who might guide you on the job.

Training programs are useful for teaching the tools of trade:

Company and product knowledge
Effective time management
Sales techniques and sale strategy
Goals

Because sales training improves sale performance, successful companies maintain on-going training programs for their sales staffs.

Let's take a closer look at these successful selling tools.

Be knowledgeable. Successful professionals know the importance of being thoroughly knowledgeable about all aspects of their businesses. Knowledge helps build confidence, and confidence in yourself and your product are essential to sales success. Further, a knowledgeable salesperson will be able to provide better service to the customer.

Time is money. Effective time management means managing your work time wisely in order to maximize profit. In a 9–5 job, discipline is built in. In sales, you provide your own discipline. Because there is only so much time in a day, and a world full of selling opportunities, the fast-track person:

Knows priorities

Organizes and plans the work day or work week.

In other words "Plan your work and work your plan."

Sales technique and selling strategy will vary with each sales opportunity. Your sales approach is critical, for early in your presentation you will want to capture your customer's interest and attention knowing your customer will help you customize your sales strategy so you can point out how your product or service will benefit *this* customer. Have a plan. Be prepared with an alternative strategy should you need to alter your plans in a specific situation. Developing a selling style that is effective for you comes with trial and error. Don't be afraid to learn and try different styles and techniques.

Finally, successful salespeople are obsessed with goals. There are immediate goals, short-term goals and long-term goals. An immediate goal might be to increase sales over last month, last quarter, last year, or to expand your customer or client base. A long-term goal might be a promotion into management. Goals give you direction; hard work, persistence, and planning will make reaching your goals possible. Set high goals early and stick to them.

UNDERSTANDING SALES

In any sales situation you are actually selling the benefits of your product or service to the buyer—that is the basis of the sale. Making a sale is a complicated process that begins long before the salesperson asks for the order.

Locating and qualifying potential customers is the first step in the sales process. Often this is called prospecting, marketing, canvassing, or cold calling. Sometimes customers will find you, but more often, you will need to find the customers. Leads and referrals are a salesperson's lifeblood. Leads are potential customers. The name of a person or business who might be a prospect is referred to as a lead. Where do you find leads? Through club memberships and associations, directories, calls to friends and colleagues, old invoices, call reports and credit and shipping records. Leads can be purchased in the form of lists from list brokers (generally listed under mailing list in the yellow pages). List brokers comply and maintain accurate lists of specific customer groups. A referral is when someone you know gives you the name of a potential customer. Referrals are the best kinds of leads. And the best way to get referrals is to ask for them. Always carry business cards. You never know when you will meet someone who could lead to a sale.

Get as much information as possible about what the prospects wants and/or needs. Of course, it is to the person who has purchasing power that you will pitch—more elegantly, "make the presentation"—so find out who that is.

Be prepared. Have all the materials you will need on hand—brochures, order forms, purchase orders, calculator. Knowing the basis of a good sales presentation, keeping it brief and to the point, and presenting it in a courteous and informative manner will help you make the sale. A good presentation will set the stage for the close.

Listen. A good sales presentation is not all talk. Listen, in order to put together a winning presentation. Listen to what the customer is saying, to the questions being asked, the needs being described, and the responses to your delivery. This will help you anticipate and overcome objections.

Here are some common barriers to your making a sale.

Knowledge of the prospect and of your products and overall sales savvy will help you overcome them:

- The prospect doesn't know what he or she needs or wants.

- The prospect doesn't know enough about your product or service to make an informed decision to purchase and so decides not to buy.

- The prospect has concerns about price or payment terms, rather than about the product or service itself.

- The prospect is already being serviced satisfactorily by a competitor.

- The prospect is "shopping" and may not be in the market at all.

After you have overcome overt objections, *ask for the order!* (This may sound obvious, but is all too often overlooked by even experienced salespeople.) Get a commitment—*today!* Once a person has signed an order or has formally committed to the sale, there is a feeling of obligation. A promise without a commitment is not enough. Experienced salespeople tell us that a promised order will probably never be a sale. Finally, close the sale. Stop talking (you don't want to talk yourself out of it!) and leave as soon as courtesy permits.

Remember that even the best salesperson doesn't make every sale. If it becomes apparent that your prospect is not buying and cannot be sold, express your thanks for the time given you and go on to the next sales opportunity.

Top salespeople know that the sale doesn't end when the order is written. Follow-up and services are an essential part of sales strategy. Be consistent in dealing with the customer and follow through on all commitments and promises. Follow-up and services create good will between salesperson and customer and will help to generate future sales.

In conclusion, there are no secrets to selling. Technique can be learned and the sales strategy can be taught.

TELEPHONE SALES

The telephone is an important business tool. Millions of dollars are made each year in telephone sales. A bank may market a new service to its customers by telephoning; you may be called and asked to purchase a magazine subscription, and so on. A telephone sales call might be to introduce yourself, your product and/or service to a prospect; to make and confirm an appointment; follow-up on an order; or to ask for a reorder. You can see that the telephone can serve a multitude of purposes.

A telephone salesperson can cover more "ground" over the telephone wires in a day than in the field in a week. A field sales call may cost $200 to $300, a telephone sales call may cost $20.

Keep your calls brief and interesting. You should be able to get your message across and qualify your prospect within a short time. You don't need to give a lot of detail over the telephone. The point is to give just enough so that the customer will want to see someone to discuss your product or service further. Of course, if the prospect expresses interest to buy immediately, close the deal! More likely your "close" by phone will be making an appointment to meet with the prospect. In any case, stress the benefits of your product or service to the customer on the telephone just the way you would if you were presenting face to face.

Be natural. Do not be intimidated by the telephone. What you need in order to sell successfully by telephone is a clear speaking voice, confidence, enthusiasm, courtesy, and the ability to project authority. Plan your telephone sales call in the same way you would if you were making your sales call presentation face to face. Use the telephone. It can save you time and make you money.

What follows are industry hot spots where sales professionals are "cleaning up."

Insurance Sales

Insurance sales offers both financial and personal rewards. Most individuals and businesses consider insurance a necessity. So for the insurance salesperson, a potential client may be the family next door or the grocery manager at the local supermarket; the mother of your daughter's playmate or the drycleaner. As is true with any kind of sales, the insurance salesperson must plan his or her time well and be creative in locating and initiating new clients with little or no supervision. Insurance sales allows for a flexible schedule in the evening and weekend for the convenience of the client.

There are two basic types of insurance: Life insurance, and property and casualty insurance.

The life insurance salesperson sells policies that are designed to provide for the financial security of others (usually family members) in the event of that person's death.

The property and casualty salesperson sells policies that protect individuals and businesses from financial loss as a result of fire or theft, automobile accidents, or other losses. It also includes all forms of liability insurance, which covers the costs if you are responsible for injury to another person or damage to someone's property.

Health insurance falls neatly into either category. These policies cover the cost of hospital and medical care, and disability.

All insurance salespeople must be licensed by the state in which they sell insurance. Applicants must pass a written exam covering insurance fundamentals and that state's insurance laws. While many employers prefer to have salespeople with a college degree, high school graduates with potential and/or proven sales ability can find rewarding jobs in the insurance industry.

Because insurance is such a complex and expensive product, the insurance sales professional must be well-informed and knowledgeable about the various policies and options available. The salesperson must also be sincere and empathetic toward the "layperson" (you and I) who knows little about this complex subject.

Most insurance salespeople are paid by commission. Commissions are paid not only on new policies but on renewals as well. The *Occupational Outlook Handbook 1986–1987* reports that it is possible for the fast-track insurance sales professional to earn $25,000 in commissions on renewals alone. Couple that income with the potential principal income policies for a fast-track salesperson, and it becomes clear how many insurance salespeople can earn $100,000 a year and more. *Money*, December 1986 reports that the average life insurance agent earns $52,600 a year. (Casualty salespeople do better!) The top producer at Northwestern Mutual Life Insurance Co. earned $300,000. What could a fast-tracking salesperson like you earn?

COMPUTER SOFTWARE SALES ————————————

Sales of software, the program or computer operating instructions needed to operate a computer, requires sophisticated sales ability, technical know-how and familiarity with computer language, all of which can be learned in the training programs offered by many software manufacturers and distributors. These training programs can be short—a few weeks, or long—9 months or more. Education and re-education of selling professionals is constant when dealing with such a high-tech, state-of-the-art type of product. Computers and programs become obsolete as soon as a newer, quicker, more sophisticated product is introduced. The required technical information includes an intimate knowledge of ideas and concepts, compatibility, information needs, speed, and price, in order to tailor a software package to the users' needs.

While corporations and institutions are buying rather sophisticated software, the retail buyers are proving that entertainment and amusement programs are widely sought-after. How-to, self-improvement, and do-it-yourself programs are big business. Customized software packages for government, health services, and professionals have had a significant impact in the marketplace.

Most successful software salespeople combine technical knowledge with how-to-sell. College is preferred and advanced degrees are helpful. Salaries of $100,000 to $300,000 are commonplace among computer sales professionals.

AUCTIONEERING

Ladies Home Journal, May 1985, reports that auctioneering is the eleventh highest paying field in the country. Surprised? We were. As we researched the field of auctioneering for this book, we learned the potential income of fast-tracking auctioneers was $100,000 + a year. Industry insiders claim good auctioneers can earn $200,000 a year or more. With only 25,000 auctioneers servicing 200 million Americans, no need to worry about competition. And surprisingly, where there are many auction houses, business is best. For example, the major galleries in New York City, Sotheby Parke Bernet, Christie's, and William Doyle will all schedule specialty auctions in the same week—buyers are in town and looking to buy.

There is no limit to what can be sold at auction. Antiques, automobiles, cattle, heavy equipment, household goods, real estate, and jewelry all have been sold at fair market value by auctioneers. Your authors have personally bought a sportscar and a piano at auction at prices well below wholesale.

What does it take to be an auctioneer? Guts and super salesmanship, perhaps even showmanship. The auctioneer needs to keep the bidding lively and the audience actively participating.

The art of auctioneering is taught at half a dozen schools

throughout the United States. One such school is the International Auction School in South Deerfield, Massachusetts. Douglas P. Bilodeau, 40, owner and president of the school, tells us his students learn every phase of auctioneering, including auction law, advertising, bookkeeping and bid calling. His students, who spend two weeks in training, go through a practical course of lectures and demonstrations. They learn voice control—how to talk from the diaphragm and not the throat. Bilodeau tells us that an auctioneer can talk for four, five, eight, even twelve hours at a time once this technique is mastered. During an auction it is the auctioneer who does *all* the talking. The buyers raise their hands, bidding paddles, or eyebrows to signal their bid to the auctioneer. The bid calling might be a chant or at the very least a rhythmic call. It might sound like this: "I'm a bid 50, now 60, now 70. G'me 80, now 90, 90 once, 90 twice, sold! For ninety dollars to number twenty-two." The bidder bids against other interested buyers until only one buyer remains, at which time the item is "knocked down" or sold to this highest bidder. The pace is fast; 120 lots could be offered in an hour, so the person who is buying must be in tune or risk losing an item. Above all, the auctioneer must be composed and remain in charge at all times.

The auctioneer's commission is generally 20 percent of the sale. Bilodeau tells us of a recent sale he ran that grossed $100,000. His commission was $20,000, he spent $2500 on advertising and expenses, leaving him with a profit of $17,500 for two days' work.

We pause here in order to point out to the reader that throughout this book, we have discussed other fast-track careers involving some form of sales: *Securities sales, advertising sales, executive search, spot television sales, and others.* Choosing to sell in any one of these industries may lead to financial independence.

You also need to recognize that the sale of the product or service in any industry is only half the sales package. The other half is you, the sales professional. At each sales call you are selling your reputation, your individual sales approach, your personal touch. Good salesmanship requires honesty, integrity, and sincerity. Manipulating customers into making bad purchasing decisions is not good salesmanship. If a sale doesn't fit a need or is something the purchaser truly can't afford—don't sell! Greedy salespeople run out of prospects surprisingly fast.

The salesperson's earnestness, quality service and follow through are what will make it likely that the customer will be back to buy from you again.

SALES: A FAST-TRACK FOR WOMEN

While sales has always been a fast-track career choice for men, women are just beginning to consider this area as a career opportunity. Within this decade sales has become the fastest growing profession for women. Women welcome the kind of financial independence and challenge a sales career can offer. Some women are taking advantage of the visibility afforded the successful salesperson in an effort to reach top management jobs. Women are being hired to sell everything from lumber to steel, from heavy machinery to computers, from pharmaceuticals to commodities and are as successful as their male counterparts.

Success-oriented women who enter sales often double and triple their previous income in short periods of time. Many are earning more than they ever dreamed possible—and loving it! One 28-year-old saleswoman we interviewed told us she is earning $60,000 a year after only eighteen months on the job. She sells long-distance telephone services.

Although success in most jobs is determined by someone else's evaluation, a salesperson's success is measured simply by a set of sales figures. Either you sell or you don't sell.

Regardless of the personal feelings of the sales manager or supervisor, your sales production is the proof that determines your success. This advantage, unique to the world of selling, is helping to eliminate the kind of prejudice towards women that has been commonplace in the corporate world.

Further, sales offers the kind of flexible work schedules that attract working mothers or the single parent. As long as you sell, and your product permits, you can do it at midday or at midnight. It needn't be nine to five, and could be part-time. If you demonstrate sales ability or are a proven producer, job requirements can be negotiated.

If you are an intelligent woman seeking a challenging job; if you are capable and willing to work hard; if you want a job with a bight future; and if you are willing to make compromises in your personal life in exchange for a chance to earn a lot of money, we encourage you to consider sales as a fast-track career choice.

SALARY VS. COMMISSION

Salespeople work either on straight salary, salary plus commission, and/or bonus or strictly commission.

Straight salary is compensated in the same way most office jobs are; an agreed-upon annual salary is paid weekly, bi-weekly, twice a month, or once a month depending on company policy. While straight salary compensation assures you of a guaranteed sum, it has a drawback—straight salary arrangements rigidly limit your earnings potential.

Salary plus commission and/or bonuses usually provide for a small base salary and a small commission arrangement. And for some this is the best of two worlds—providing an incentive and a secure income. However, too often the commission or bonus is based on group production (or net commission). In other words, all the salespeople on the "team" share in the override, regardless of effort and ability. If you are the superstar on the team, salary plus will likely cost you earnings. Here again, income potential is an issue that is compromised by assuring the salesperson a minimum income. It is not likely that the experienced or fast-tracking sales professional will recognize his or her greatest earnings potential working on a salary plus commission basis.

The successful salesperson opts to work on a straight commission basis where the sky's the limit. Harder work and more effective selling strategies earn more money for this salesperson. The commission structure provides an incentive to work hard and the salesperson's income directly reflects that hard work and effectiveness. There is some risk involved in working on commission; your income could vary sharply. Nevertheless, the majority of fast-track salespeople we interviewed indicated they would bet on themselves and opt to earn straight commissions.

A salesperson working on straight commission may anticipate future income and may draw a weekly or biweekly "paycheck"—a certain amount of money against future commissions. This makes it possible to budget and balance one's financial life without waiting for that big commission check, which may be paid only monthly or even quarterly.

Earnings Overview

Sales pays well! The wealthiest people in this country are not doctors and lawyers—they are salespeople who have made good. They are the sales force of America, out earning megabucks. According to the National Association for Professional Saleswomen, of all people who earn $50,000 or more in this country, 65 percent are in sales.

Good salespeople are in great demand in every industry. We know of no other field in which recognition and reward can come as quickly. No need to guess at the value of a salesperson—his or her sales record tells just what he or she is accomplishing.

The financial rewards of a sales career compare to none. Men and women like yourselves are earning the kind of money dreams are made of. Why not you?

GLOSSARY

Call Report:
A report of names of people, companies and other relevant information the salesperson writes up in order to keep track of who was contacted, where and when, and what took place.

Close:
The end result of your presentation asking for the sale.

Commission:
An agreed upon percentage of the sale paid to the salesperson. No doubt about it, those who sell the most, earn the most.

Draw (against commission):
An agreed upon salary which will be deducted from future earnings.

Effective Time Management:
The art of using your work time wisely in order to produce the greater number of sales.

Lead:
The name of a person or business who might be a potential customer.

List Broker:
A person or company that compiles and maintains lists of specific customer groups (you'll find these in the classified phone directory under "Mailing Lists").

Objections:
Reasons why a prospective customer can't or won't buy.

Override:
Bonus, usually based on an overall percentage of sales.

Pitch: (verb)
To present, to sell.

Presentation:
A well-planned sales proposal highlighting the benefits of the product or service to the customer.

Prospect:
A potential customer or client.

Prospecting:
The art of locating and qualifying potential customers.

Referral:
The name of a potential customer given to you by someone who knows both of you. Referrals are the best kind of leads.

Salary Plus Commission:
A base salary and generally a small commission. For some salespeople this offers security and still provides the extra motivation that commissions provide.

Self Starter:
Confident, independent, determined and motivated individual who needs little supervision.

Straight Salary:
An agreed upon annual salary without any added incentive.

WHAT YOU SHOULD BE READING

Career Guide for Sales and Marketing
William Lewis and Hal Cornelius
Monarch Press, NY, 1983

Computer World
P.O. Box 880
Framingham, MA 01701

Datamation
875 Third Avenue
New York, NY 10022

Personal Selling Power
Gerhard, Gschwandtner & Associates
P.O. Box 5467
Fredericksburg, VA 22403

Sales and Marketing Management Magazine
Bill Communications, Inc.

P.O. Box 1042
Southeast, PA 19398-9900

ORGANIZATIONS FOR MORE INFORMATION ——

American Marketing Association
250 South Wacker Drive
Chicago, IL 60606

The College of Insurance
101 Murray Street
New York, NY 10007

Cooperative Association of Professional Salespeople
2120 S. Green Road, Suite 210
South Euclid, OH 44121

Dartnell Institute
4660 Ravenswood Avenue
Chicago, IL 60640

Insurance Information Institute
110 William Street
New York, NY 10038

National Association for Professional Saleswomen (NAPS)
2088 Morley Way
Sacramento, CA 95825

The National Auctioneer Association
800 Ballentine
Overland Park, Kansas 66214

Sales Executives Club of New York
122 East 42nd Street
New York, NY 10017

Sales Manpower Foundation
122 East 42nd Street
New York, NY 10168

Sales & Marketing Executives International
380 Lexington Avenue
New York, NY 10168

8

HOSPITALITY
Luxury Living Comes of Age

The hospitality industry—restaurants, hotels, and allied businesses—is expected to be one of the largest and fastest growing through the end of the century. Higher average income and more leisure time will allow the buying public to eat out more often and to travel more frequently. Good jobs are waiting for interested and qualified applicants. Training is available on the job and salaries (including bonuses and fringes) are handsome.

The hospitality industry is perhaps the ultimate service industry catering to the comforts and palates of an ever discriminating traveling and dining public. Long hours and frequent weekend and holiday work are commonplace in this service-oriented business. Most hotels and motels operate 24 hours a day, 7 days a week, 365 days a year. Restaurants have more limited operating hours.

Commercial hotels/motels and restaurants account for 85 percent of all industry sales. And we're talking about big business—30 billion dollars worth. In fact, the hospitality industry is the sixth largest industry in the nation.

Hotel/motel management and restaurant/food service operations make up this broad-based industry. In order to draw a clear picture of these fast-track career opportunities, we will discuss them separately.

THE RESTAURANT BUSINESS

Also known as the food service industry, the restaurant business is the number one retail employer in the United States. According to the National Restaurant Association, it is the third largest business in the United States. New restaurants and bars open in response to population growth and increased spending for food and drink outside the home. As women continue to work outside the home in increasing numbers, families are finding dining out a welcome convenience.

A person considering a career in the restaurant business has several investment options:

• Managing a restaurant for someone else.
• Purchasing a franchise and operating a franchise restaurant.
• Buying an existing restaurant.
• Building a new restaurant and operating it.

Managing a restaurant for someone else eliminates all financial risks and can be well paying, but the opportunity for earning megabucks is very limited. This position could be an intermediate stone towards future ownership.

Buying a franchise may be expensive, but it reduces the risk of failure. Almost all franchises offer a complete training course to franchisees before they open their restaurant. A franchiser's good reputation (perhaps national) and excellent track record can almost guarantee success. Of course, as with any franchise situation, the big trade-off is the limited input you have into management and design.

Buying an existing restaurant can be less expensive than

building a new restaurant establishment, but beware. It is essential you determine the real reason that the business is for sale.

If the owner's poor health or retirement is the reason for the sale, and the business is priced right, this might be an ideal purchase. However, if business is declining or the neighborhood is changing or the lease is expiring, you may be buying trouble. Let caution be your guide, along with a good accountant and a good lawyer.

Building a new restaurant and operating it demands *big* bucks, business and restaurant experience, and careful planning. Begin with the basics:

- What kind of food will be served?
- What will the price range be?
- What type of service will be offered?
- What kind of atmosphere, decor?

Operating expenses, breakeven figures, and start-up costs must all be considered. The menu, including kinds of food and price, the decor and ambiance, and the type of service you provide will all determine your clientele.

After a suitable concept has been decided upon, a suitable site must be found. (Sometimes the concept is not suitable to the site. It seems easier to alter the kind of restaurant than to pass on a suitable site.) In order to determine if a real demand for a particular kind of restaurant exists at that location, or if there is an oversupply of similar restaurants nearby, contact the Conference Board in New York City. They publish annually a *Consensus of Selected Service Industries* which reports on the number of establishments in an area and their total receipts and payroll. This information, coupled with an indepth market evaluation, can be a valuable resource when choosing a site. Be aware that a restaurant's success depends primarily on its location.

Where Shall We Dine?

The three main segments of the food service industry are commercial, institutional, and military. For our purpose of exploring fast-track career opportunities in the 1990s, we are focusing on commercial service only. Your local library could supply you with information on institutional and military food service.

Commercial establishments are open to the public and are for-profit operations. They account for 85 percent of all industry sales. Included in this category are restaurants, food service contractors (for example, airline food suppliers), hotel and motel restaurants, and restaurants in department stores, drugstores, etc.

Specifically, there are five types of restaurants, each offering a different dining experience:

- *Family Style Restaurant.* Unpretentious and casual. Modestly priced and providing relatively fast service. Frequented by families.
- *Atmosphere Restaurant.* Ambiance and decor is a big draw. Usually modestly priced.
- *Gourmet Restaurant.* Emphasis on exquisitely prepared food. Sophisticated menu. Gracious atmosphere and leisurely dining.
- *Fast Food Restaurant.* Limited and inexpensive menu. Fast service and convenient. Often chain or franchise.
- *Take Out Restaurant.* Eat-out-at-home is newest and biggest trend in restaurant service. Already prepared foods are picked up or delivered for consumption at home.

One operation is not necessarily more successful than the other but different skills are required for successful operation of different types of restaurants. Location counts. Be sure to choose a suitable style of restaurant for its location and likely patrons.

In the Kitchen

The prestige that has been awarded European chefs for years has finally traveled overseas. Chefs in America are now recognized professionals. Cooking is no longer regarded as a blue-collar job. In fact, a chef is recognized not simply as an excellent cook, but also as a highly skilled, well-trained business person who coordinates, supervises, and participates in all kitchen functions, including preparing, ordering, and selecting food items.

The chef is in charge of the entire kitchen operation (often called the "heart of the restaurant"), responsible not only for food preparation and presentation, but also the control of waste and throwaway. Tight kitchen control is essential for success in the restaurant business. The chef might be compared to a plant manager in an industrial factory—the one in charge of plant operation and output.

Getting a Job

According to the Bureau of Labor Statistics there will be at least a 50 percent increase in the demand for chefs through 1995. Some of the larger restaurant chains recruit right off campus. But if you aren't lucky enough to get into a training program, don't despair. Opportunities are plentiful. Word of mouth is a great way to hear about job opportunities. Professional associations, classified ads, trade magazines, and professional journals all provide information on job opportunities. Be prepared to start at the bottom, but rest assured, for those hard-working and dedicated professionals, career advancement comes quickly in the restaurant field.

Culinary Education and Training ⸻

Employers prefer applicants with high school educations who have completed advanced training at a vocational or specialty school. College graduates with degrees in restaurant management are sought after.

Further, graduates of restaurant management and/or culinary art schools are almost certain to get a job—and a good one. Those that graduate from one of the renowned programs such as:

- Cornell University, School of Hotel Administration, Ithaca, NY
- Michigan State University, School of Hotel, Restaurant and Institutional Management, East Lansing, MI
- The Culinary Institute of America, Hyde Park, NY

These schools have four or five apprenticeships to choose from. Often two or three years of apprenticeship are necessary in order to qualify for the job of chef.

There are more than one hundred four-year colleges that award degrees in restaurant and hotel management. The course of study is diversified. Some of the courses one might study are:

Food purchasing and storage

Food preparation

Menu planning

Equipment purchase and layout

Personnel management

Nutrition

Beverage control

Sanitation and safety

Food cost accounting

The cost of training a chef can be considerable. Tuition at the Culinary Institute of America, Hyde Park, NY can run $12,000 or more for a full 21-month academic program. And the admissions office reports having to turn away applicants.

Earning Power

Many food service operations are willing to train on the job. So while advanced education is helpful to getting on the fast track in the restaurant business, the high school graduate with ambition can start in low gear and work up. Most employers feel that experience is the best teacher.

While there are good paying jobs within a restaurant, perhaps the fast track for manager or chef alike would be to own one's own restaurant. Just about everyone has at some time fantasized about owning an attractive, profitable little restaurant (especially those who like to dine out), but operating a restaurant is not an easy job. Approximately *80 percent* of all restaurants fail after only one year—a startling statistic that might and should discourage the meek. But the entrepreneurial person with the dream of a restaurant is hardly discouraged. Forewarned, Yes! Cautioned, Yes! Discouraged, No!

Leave *nothing* to chance. A well-planned, well-managed, well-staffed restaurant has potential for great success. Successful restaurants can show sizeable profits, and can make their owners or investors financially independent but the risks are high.

THE HOTEL/MOTEL BUSINESS

The hotel/motel provides a variety of services based on the clientele it wishes to attract. Some of these services are obvious: a clean room, good food, television. Other services are more specialized: health facility and year-round swimming pool, stenographic services, notary public, library, valet service, entertainment, children's nursery, convention halls, meeting rooms and banquets.

Generally speaking, there are three types of hotel/motel operations:

Commercial

Residential

Resort

Commercial hotels, like commercial restaurants, make up three-quarters of the hotels/motels in this country. They cater to the commercial traveler, the business person, salesperson, transient visitor and tourist trade. Much of their revenue comes from the convention and business meeting. In fact, hotels and motels without meeting and banquet facilities operate at a disadvantage.

Residential hotels provide permanent and semi-permanent living quarters for their quests. Some of the better known hotels, such as the Westin Plaza and the Waldorf Astoria in New York, rent a large number of suites on a permanent basis. They offer housekeeping services, room service, and dining facilities to their permanent residents—amenities these guests would not get in an ordinary apartment.

The hotel/motel business is a people business. Cleanliness, cost control, and good people relations are critical to success. A central location, convenient to the airport, highway and main thoroughfare is essential. While the tourist trade makes up approximately one third of all hotel/motel business, the majority of the lodging business comes from the business traveler.

Resort hotels provide food and lodging plus sports and meeting facilities. Some resort hotels are built on acres of land surrounded by golf courses, tennis courts, swimming and boating facilities, and more. Some offer planned social activities and entertainment, while others offer none at all, just guaranteed solitude, uninterrupted quiet.

Hotel/Motel Ownership

Because of the high cost of hotel/motel development, many hotels are owned by large financial institutions, insurance companies, or real estate investment syndicates. At the individual level, one might get a group of friends together to buy or build or manage a hotel; or one could lease a hotel/motel and pay the owner a percentage of sales. In any case, business know-how and access to money are a given. Note that often the greatest profit does not come from lodging, food, or beverage sales, but from the real estate value or tax benefits afforded its owners or investors.

Hotel/Motel Management

If you choose to pursue a career in the hospitality industry and the thought of hotel/motel ownership is enticing, you might consider hotel/motel management. Over the years, management personnel have been comparatively well paid. The best paying management jobs are:

- Chef
- General manager
- Food and beverage manager (including banquet & catering)
- Manager of sales (including convention, meetings & tour bookings)

We have already reviewed the fast-track career of the chef. Now let's consider the career opportunities of the hotel manager, food and beverage manager and the manager of sales.

General Manager

The hotel/motel manager is responsible for coordinating all functioning areas of the hotel. This includes, housekeeping and maintenance, food and beverage service, pricing policies, personnel matters, advertising, and publicity. In larger operations, the manager employs a staff who work closely with him or her in order to ensure an efficient and profitable operation. In smaller hotels or motels, the manager wears many hats and may be directly responsible for some of these jobs.

The manager must have good business sense, leadership ability, be good with people, and have lots of energy. The job often requires long hours, nights, and weekend work.

General managers earn upwards of $100,000 a year plus fringes. Executive vice presidents and managers of major hotel chains earn as much as $175,000–$280,000 annually.

Food and Beverage Manager

The food and beverage manager is in charge of all services dealing with the purchase and serving of food and beverages. This may include supervision of several restaurants, banquet rooms, coffee shops, cocktail lounges, and nightclubs. The food and beverage manager must carefully monitor all purchases of foods and liquors. He or she must know the number of times each dish on the menu is ordered, the economy of preparing each dish again, and how leftovers may be used. The cost of preparing meals and serving drinks is figured down to the smallest fraction. It is the food and beverage manager who analyzes the kitchen operation taking into account quantity and quality, the relation between food and labor costs, and price changes for the menu.

Further, the food and beverage manager oversees the banquet and catering department. In many hotels, banquets and catering functions contribute in a large way to the profit of the business. The manager's compensation is handsome and often includes free meals.

Manager of Sales

Convention sales, meetings, and tour group bookings provide some hotels/motels with more than half their annual income. Cities like New York, Atlanta, Chicago, Miami, Dallas, Boston, and San Francisco even have special bureaus to solicit convention business. It is no surprise that the manager of sales holds a key position.

The manager of sales must be able to communicate well in order to promote the use of the hotel's facilities and services. The manager coordinates all the activities and plans for people to work behind the scenes to ensure that everything runs smoothly. Some of the services negotiated by the convention or tour operator with the hotel sales manager may include: transportation, entertainment, easy registration and check out, and meals. Often the sales manager solicits business from state and national businesses, organizations, and associations. Most convention sites are selected from one to five years in advance. The most popular sites are booked as far as ten years in advance.

If fast-tracking in hotel sales interests you, you should direct your education toward learning about food service and hotel management. If that is not possible, be prepared to start either at the front desk or in the kitchen. Opportunity is yours, and your advancement will depend upon your ability, ambition, and desire to succeed.

Profile

Jay Pivnick
Hotel Owner/Operator, Glen Paul's Financial, Inc.,
Paramus, New Jersey

After handling years of real estate investments (apartment buildings, office buildings and shopping centers) Pivnick and his associates acquired two Florida properties that were hotel/motel franchises—one Ramada Inn, the other a Days-Inn. Both were small (approximately 140 rooms), relatively simple to run operations.

Glen Paul's Properties acts as the absentee management company for Pivnick's hotels/motels. Pivnick tells us, "We employ a field staff as well as on-site personnel. All operation decisions are made from the home office. We prepare our budgets early in the year and the managers at each property are expected to live within the framework of that budget. Our on-site managers are key personnel. They oversee the day-to-day operation of our hotels and we depend on them a great deal."

The hospitality business is a people business. Pivnick says, "It is just an extension of how you treat guests in your home. We work hard at, and encourage our staff to work hard at keeping guest satisfaction high."

We asked Pivnick if a hotel/motel management degree was essential to success in his operation. He responded, "Although the classroom experience is helpful, there is nothing that beats hands-on experience. Graduates from the top hotel/motel management programs are sought after by franchise companies to hold positions in the company, but in the field, it's a different story. You learn in three months on the job more than you do in four or six years in college. We pay for experience."

Pivnick tells us he finds hotel/motel management challenging, exciting, and profitable. He warns anyone interested in the business to be very selective when setting out to acquire hotel property. "Certified accounting statements are helpful," he says, "but they don't tell you about the staff, the general labor market in the area, the type of customer. It's hard to tell if the property is going to produce cash flow until you're there operating it. Investigate carefully, and research! You can't do enough of that."

Pivnick has great plans for the future of Glen Paul's Properties. Short term (18 months or so), they plan on doubling their size. For the future he tells us, "I believe we will be developing our own properties and possibly establish our own franchise." His fantasy: "To retire young. In this business one can retire young and continue to live very well."

Education and Training

The front desk, the kitchen, or housekeeping (believe it or not) are excellent starting places for young professionals interested in growth opportunities. A second language is helpful, particularly if seeking employment with an international chain or franchise.

Lack of education is not a barrier to employment in the lodging industry but it does determine where you begin your career. High school is essential and college is preferred. It seems that larger hotels and motels give preference to those applicants who have completed coursework in hotel management or who have been awarded degrees in hotel/motel administration from the many colleges offering the specialized program. A bachelor's degree in hotel administration does provide a particularly strong preparation for a career in hotel management. (See the listing at the end of this chapter of selected schools offering programs in Food Management and Hotel Administration. A comprehensive list of schools offering hotel management courses and degrees is available through the Council on Hotel, Restaurant and Institutional Education, 11 Kroger Center, Suite 219, Norfolk, VA 23502. Some of the larger chains have special training programs. If interested, do apply. Good Luck!

GLOSSARY

Booking:
Reservation.

Chef:
A well-trained businessperson responsible for food preparation and monitoring kitchen functions and supplies.

Eat-Out-at-Home:
Store bought, catered, or prepared foods purchased to eat at home.

Food Service Industry:
The industry that services and caters to an eating public in restaurants, snack bars and/or convention halls.

Food Cost Accounting:
The procedure used to determine and control the actual cost of a food item considering waste, perishability and other related factors.

Front Desk:
Check in and check out point of hotel/motel. Usually responsible for all complaints.

Hospitality Industry:
Includes all services rendered to the public as in restaurants, hotels and motels.

House:
A synonym for hotel used commonly in the industry.

WHAT YOU SHOULD BE READING

Cooking for Profit
Gas Magazines, Inc.
1202 Park Street
Madison, WI 53715

Food Management
Harcourt, Brace, Jovonovich, Inc.
757 Third Avenue
New York, NY 10017

Food Service Marketing
2132 Fordem Avenue
Box 7158
Madison, WI 53707

Hospitality
Penton/IPC Publications
111 Chester Avenue
Cleveland, OH 44114

Hotel and Motel Management
Robert Freeman Publishing Company
1713 Central Street
Evanston, IL 60201

Hotel and Motel Red Book
American Hotel Association Directory Corporation
888 Seventh Avenue
New York, NY 10019

Lodging and Food Service News
Hotel Service Inc.
755 Boylston Street
Boston, MA 02116

Nation's Restaurant News
425 Park Avenue
New York, NY 10022

Resort Management
Resort Management, Inc.
1509 Madison Avenue
P.O. Box 4169
Memphis, TN 38104

Restaurant Business
633 Third Avenue
New York, NY 10017

Restaurant Hospitality
1111 Chester Avenue
Cleveland, OH 44114

Restaurants and Institutions
5 South Wabash Avenue
Chicago, IL 60603

ORGANIZATIONS FOR MORE INFORMATION ——

American Culinary Federation
P.O. Box 3466
St. Augustine, FL 32084

The American Hotel and Motel Association
888 Seventh Avenue
New York, NY 10019

Directory of Hotel and Restaurant Schools
Council on Hotel, Restaurant and Institutional Education
Henderson Human Development Building, Rm 12
The Pennsylvania State University
University Park, PA 16802

The Education Institute of American Hotel and Motel Associations
1107 S. Harrison Road
East Lansing, MI 48823

National Institute for the Foodservice Industry
20 North Wacker Drive
Chicago, IL 60606

National Restaurant Association
Information Service and Library
311 First Street, N.W.
Washington, DC 20001

Small Business Bibliography—Motels
Small Business Administration
Publication No. 66
Washington, DC 20001

SELECTED SCHOOLS OFFERING PROGRAMS IN FOOD SERVICE AND HOTEL MANAGEMENT ——

Baltimore Institute of Culinary Arts
19 South Gay Street
Baltimore, MD 21201

Cornell University
School of Hotel Administration
Statler Hall
Ithaca, NY 14853

The Culinary Institute of America
Culinary Arts
P.O. Box 53
Hyde Park, NY 12538

Florida International University
School of Hotel, Food and Travel Services
Miami, FL 33199

Johnson and Wales College
Hospitality Management
8 Abbott Park Place
Providence, RI 02903

Michigan State University
School of Hotel Restaurant and Institutional Management
424 Eppley Center
East Lansing, MI 48824

Pratt Institute
Department of Nutrition and Dietetics
215 Ryerson Street
Room 406 Dekalb Hall
Brooklyn, NY 11205

The University of New Hampshire
Hotel Administration Program
Mc Connell Hall
Durham, NH 03824

University of Denver
School of Hotel and Restaurant Management
2030 East Evans
Denver, CO 80208

9

ENTREPRENEURS
The New Breed

Webster's dictionary defines an entrepreneur as *one who organizes and directs a business, assuming the risks for the sake of profits.* Entrepreneurs are "no guts, no glory" people. This type of career is an alternative for fast-trackers who want both maximum control and maximum income. It involves more risk taking than any other career choice in this book, and if our research is correct, it also guarantees the greatest amount of self satisfaction. As an entrepreneur, you are the one who has the power and tenacity to make an idea a reality.

DO I QUALIFY FOR THE JOB?

Successful entrepreneurs come in all shapes and sizes. They come from all walks of life and diverse educational backgrounds. Some have years of business experience, some have none. Some possess multiple or advanced degrees and still others have never been to or finished college.

Just having a dream or a business vision doesn't ensure your success. Fast-track entrepreneurs are a special breed of people with some traits in common. These include:

- Their idea is an obsession. The belief in their product or service is so strong that they couldn't perceive failure.

- They have need to control and be one's own boss.

- They have foresight and perceive the opportunity to achieve tremendous financial success.

- They possess courage and confidence. Entrepreneurs can't have one without the other. They are adventurers willing to risk.

- They have an optimistic and often idealistic outlook. Some entrepreneurs are accused of being naive (and it works in their favor). They didn't know it couldn't be done, so they did it!

- An immunity to the word "No" is part of their makeup. It is neither an obstacle nor an alternative.

- They exhibit creativity. They find a new angle or an innovative approach to an old theme and make it work in today's economy and culture.

- They are workaholics who thrive on hard work. Like all fast-trackers, entrepreneurs don't mind rolling up their sleeves.

- They have luck. This is a nontangible factor and you can't capture it no matter how hard you may try. Sometimes being in the right place at the right time *is* enough.

WHERE TO BEGIN?

If you have all of the listed traits and perhaps you are dissatisfied with your present job status, or you hate playing office politics, or maybe you simply need more control, you are ripe for your own business. If you don't know where to begin, ask yourself two basic questions:

- What am I good at?
- What do I like to do?

No entrepreneur has a chance at even a glimmer of success without being good at the pursuit to be undertaken and worse, without liking it. Once you can positively answer these two questions, you have developed your own entrepreneurial roots.

I Love My Job!

More often than not, if you like what you are doing, you are probably good at it. If the telephone is your thing, consider telephone soliciting or telemarketing. We encountered one woman in the personnel placement field who in her youth sold everything from magazines to basement waterproofing by telephone. As she settled into her highly telephone-oriented career as a placement manager, she commented that she never thought she could earn so much money telephone soliciting. It was something she both enjoyed and was good at.

If you are a fitness advocate, you are right up there with the ten most sought-after services in the 1980s and 90s. Physical health and well-being is the fair-haired child of the future. Why not propel your enthusiasm and stamina in the same way Jack La Lanne did in the 70s? Think of the fortune Jane Fonda amassed from her workout video alone. Take a look at your local health club and consider its enrollment. Why not gear yourself toward the older client or preschooler? One entrepreneur built a fortune by creating a workout video for pregnant women! Gymboree and Play-a-rena are two mini gyms for the mini person . . . and they are now franchising. As you can see, the prospects are endless.

What is important to note as you read through this chapter on entrepreneurs is that these successful business people are all doing something they like. That may seem like a reward in itself, but when you combine it with financial independence and hefty profits, you have a powerful aphrodisiac for fast-trackers.

It takes guts to leave a secure job with an assured income. You must believe in yourself and your vision. As an entrepreneur's business grows, potential investors are attracted. If you can recognize an opportunity, get others to believe in it and then take it to its limit, you are a true entrepreneur. The fast-track entrepreneur thinks: SUCCESS. Our studies show that if you believe it can be done, it probably can.

THE ENTREPRENEUR'S QUIZ

Take a few minutes to take the Center for Entrepreneurial Management's* quiz for measuring the success ratio for potential entrepreneurs.

Circle the appropriate answer.

1. How were your parents employed?
   a. Both were self-employed most of their working lives.
   b. Both were self-employed for some part of their working lives.
   c. One parent was self-employed for most of his or her working life.
   d. One parent was self-employed at some point in his or her working life.
   e. Neither parent was ever self-employed.
2. Have you ever been fired from a job?
   a. Yes, more than once.
   b. Yes, once.
   c. No.
3. What is your family background?
   a. You were born outside the United States.
   b. One or both parents were born outside the United States.

*Copyright © 1983 Joseph R. Mancuso, founder and president of Center for Entrepreneurial Management. Reprinted by permission.

    c. At least one grandparent was born outside the United States.

    d. Your grandparents, parents and you were born in the United States.

4. Describe your work career.

    a. Primarily in small business (under 100 employees).

    b. Primarily in medium-sized business (100 to 500 employees).

    c. Primarily in big business (over 500 employees).

5. Did you operate any businesses before you were 20?

    a. Many.

    b. A few.

    c. None.

6. What is your present age?

    a. 21 to 30.

    b. 31 to 40.

    c. 41 to 50.

    d. 51 or over.

7. You are the _____ child in the family?

    a. First child.

    b. Middle.

    c. Youngest.

    d. Other (foster, adopted).

8. You are:

    a. Married.

    b. Divorced.

    c. Single.

9. Your highest level of formal education is:

    a. Some high school.

    b. High school diploma.

    c. Bachelor's degree.

    d. Master's degree.

    e. Doctorate.

10. What is your primary motivation in starting a business?

    a. To make money.

    b. You don't like working for someone else.

    c. To be famous.

    d. As an outlet for excess energy.

11. Describe your relationship to the parent who provided most of the family's income.

    a. Strained.

    b. Comfortable.

    c. Competitive.

    d. Nonexistent.

12. If you had to choose between working hard or working smart, you would:

    a. Work hard.

    b. Work smart.

    c. Both.

13. On whom do you rely for critical management advice?

    a. Internal management teams.

    b. External management professionals.

    c. External financial professionals.

    d. No one except yourself.

14. If you were at the racetrack, which would you bet on?

    a. The daily double—a chance to make a killing.

    b. A 10-to-1 shot.

    c. A 3-to-1 shot.

    d. The 2-to-1 favorite.

15. The only ingredient that is both necessary and sufficient for starting a business is:

    a. Money.

    b. Customers.

    c. An idea or product.

    d. Motivation and hard work.

16. If you were an advanced tennis player and had a chance to play a top pro like Jimmy Connors, you would:

    a. Turn it down because he could easily beat you.

    b. Accept the challenge but not bet any money on it.

    c. Bet a week's pay that you would win.

    d. Get odds, bet a fortune and try for an upset.

17. You tend to fall in love too quickly with:

    a. New product ideas.

    b. New employees.

    c. New manufacturing ideas.

    d. New financial plans.

    e. All of the above.

18. Which of the following personality types is best suited to be your right-hand person?

    a. Bright and energetic.

    b. Bright and lazy.

    c. Dumb and energetic.

19. You accomplish tasks better because:

    a. You are always on time.

b. You are superorganized.

c. You keep good records.

20. You hate to discuss:
    a. Problems involving employees.
    b. Signing expense accounts.
    c. New management practices.
    d. The future of the business.

21. Given a choice, you would prefer:
    a. Rolling dice with a 1-in-3 chance of winning.
    b. Working on a problem with a 1-in-3 chance of solving it in a set time.

22. If you could choose, between the following competitive professions, it would be:
    a. Professional golf.
    b. Sales.
    c. Personnel counseling.
    d. Teaching.

23. Would you rather work with a partner who is a close friend or work with a stranger who is an expert in your field?
    a. The close friend.
    b. The expert.

24. You enjoy being with people:
    a. When you have something meaningful to do.
    b. When you can do something new and different.
    c. Even when you have nothing planned.

25. In business situations that demand action, clarifying who is in charge will help produce results.
    a. Agree.
    b. Agree with reservations.
    c. Disagree.

26. In playing a competitive game, you are concerned with:
    a. How well you play.
    b. Winning or losing.
    c. Both.
    d. Neither.

Scoring

To determine your entrepreneurial profile, find the score for each of your answers on the following chart. Add them up for your total score.

1. a = 10	b = 6	c = 5	d = 2	e = 0
2. a = 10	b = 7	c = 0		
3. a = 5	b = 4	c = 3	d = 0	
4. a = 10	b = 5	c = 0		
5. a = 10	b = 7	c = 0		
6. a = 8	b = 10	c = 5	d = 2	
7. a = 15	b = 2	c = 0	d = 0	
8. a = 10	b = 2	c = 2		
9. a = 2	b = 3	c = 10	d = 8	e = 4
10. a = 0	b = 15	c = 0	d = 0	
11. a = 10	b = 5	c = 10	d = 5	
12. a = 0	b = 5	c = 10		
13. a = 0	b = 10	c = 0	d = 5	
14. a = 0	b = 2	c = 10	d = 3	
15. a = 0	b = 10	c = 0	d = 0	
16. a = 0	b = 10	c = 3	d = 0	
17. a = 5	b = 5	c = 5	d = 5	e = 15
18. a = 2	b = 10	c = 0		
19. a = 5	b = 15	c = 5		
20. a = 8	b = 10	c = 0	d = 0	
21. a = 0	b = 15			
22. a = 3	b = 10	c = 0	d = 0	
23. a = 0	b = 10			
24. a = 3	b = 3	c = 10		
25. a = 10	b = 2	c = 0		
26. a = 8	b = 10	c = 16	d = 0	

How does your score stack up? See below:

Total Score

235–285   Successful Entrepreneur. Someone who starts multiple businesses successfully.

200–234   Entrepreneur. Starts one business successfully.

185–199   Latent Entrepreneur. Always wanted to start a business.

170–184   Potential Entrepreneur. Has the ability but has not started thinking about starting a business yet.

155–169   Borderline Entrepreneur. No qualifications but still in the running. Would need a lot of training to succeed.

Below 154   Hired Hand.

The average score for the entrepreneurs in the CEM survey is 239. CEM found that entrepreneurs often come from homes where one parent was self-employed for most of his or her working life. Many had been enterprising as youngsters—working a paper route, for example. Nearly 60 percent are the oldest child in the family and more than 75 percent are married. Fifty-six percent said they wanted to start a business primarily because they disliked working for others.

DEVELOPING A STRATEGY

Define a strategy and commit it to paper. Your business plans should include:

- Objectives/goals—short-term and long-range
- Strategies—for reaching your goals along the way
- Priorities—what's important today, tomorrow, or next year (What do I want out of this business?)
- Schedule and timetable
- Financial guidelines—prepare a budget and live by it.

The fast-trackers we spoke with all had an idea and mapped it out. They started small. They envisioned a future and they looked to expand.

Profile

William Lewis, 40
Entrepreneur

Bill Lewis is an author, the owner of a multimillion dollar personnel service, and the president of the New York School of Umpiring, the nation's only accredited training facility for baseball officials.

As a graduate of City College, "Barely," he admits, Lewis

went to work in the family business, a small, nice, prestigious employment agency that was near bankruptcy. He worked as a "gofer," learning the business from the bottom up. Says Lewis, "Four years later my mother retired and left me in charge. Driven by a brilliant father and an enterprising mother I was determined to succeed—to 'get rich' with the business." He slowly began building his dream by adding personnel counselors, a few at a time. As his revenues and business grew, Lewis was able to sell two of his five personnel divisions to an H & R Block Company in a multimillion dollar deal so that he would finally "have enough money in the bank" and "never have to worry." He is proud that his company, Career Blazers, has been twice named to Inc. magazine's list of the 100 fastest growing privately owned companies in the nation.

Lewis credits 60 percent of his success to a business consultant he hired who taught him to develop people and create systems more important than oneself. "You have to make every effort to eliminate bottlenecks and unnecessary paper, people and products that get in the way of growth." Lewis adds that today his success depends on, "good people, good planning, and good organization."

"Everywhere you look there are businesses making their owners rich." Lewis advises, "Work for someone who knows how to do it. See how they're doing it and then be creative on your own. Hopefully, you're hungry and creative, and you really want it so you work at it."

YOUR OWN BUSINESS OR OURS

Until now, for purposes of simplicity, we have assumed you are starting your own business. At this time, we would like to explore other ways of establishing business ownership. We will examine with you:

- Buying an existing business
- Purchasing a franchise

Buying an Existing Business ————————————

Some fast-trackers we spoke with considered buying an existing business the safest and easiest way into entrepreneurship. If this is the track you choose, use this outline as a guide:

1. Be sure to investigate the existing business thoroughly. Perhaps the most important ingredient will be the lease. Examine it carefully and objectively. Consider:

   - The length and terms of the remaining lease
   - Is there a renewal option?
   - Is the lease transferable or assignable?
   - Does the lease contain any unusual "use clauses" or limitations?

2. You will want to see the inventory. Consider:

   - How much inventory is there?
   - Is it up to date?
   - Has it been represented accurately?
   - Consider the fixtures and equipment. How will they figure into the overall value of the business?

3. Determine if the asking price is reasonable. Of course you'll need to consider such tangibles as the lease, the inventory and fixtures. You will examine the books (records) of the business as they exist to determine the profitability of the business.

4. Evaluate the goodwill in the business. Although the balance sheet doesn't clearly measure the profitability of goodwill, goodwill does affect the bottom line.

5. Finally, look for a motivated seller. A *must* sell situation might be:

- Retirement
- Illness
- Divorce

Understanding the needs of the seller will aid you as you negotiate the best possible purchase price. Be patient.

Franchising

The International Franchise Association defines a franchise as, "A continuing relationship in which the franchisor provides a licensed privilege to do business, plus assistance in organizing, training, merchandising, and management in return for consideration from the franchisee." In addition, the franchisor generally selects the site, offers territorial protection, and often advertises under a nationally recognized name.

The survival rate of franchises is impressive. Only two to four percent of all franchisees fail. Compare that to the rate at which other small businesses fail (as high as 50 percent over a 36-month period) and we'd say that buying a franchise could be an attractive alternative. You are, after all, buying into a proven concept.

But these "safety" features come with a price tag. As a franchisee, you lose a certain amount of control, flexibility, and creativity. You are limited to the product line or service you can offer. Franchises tend to be expensive. Also, as part of the franchise agreement, you are obliged to pay a "royalty fee" to the franchisor. This fee can be anywhere from 2 percent to 6 percent of gross annual sales, (paid monthly). Some think this is a small price to pay for the reduced risk and potential earning power a franchise income affords them.

The franchise owners we spoke to were generally satisfied. One owned a local McDonalds franchise bought ten years ago. He told us it wasn't unusual to own more than one franchise and that at age 39, he had three. We asked him how he felt about giving up so much control. He assured us he was happy with the product line, and that support from "Big Brother" was the most valued ingredient. He explained that he makes most of the day-to-day operating decisions though he does follow some regulated guidelines.

Industry statistics tell us that franchising is playing a prominent role in our entrepreneurial economy today and that it will continue to be a major alternative through the 1980s and beyond.

If you are interested in specific franchise information, call or write for the company's franchise information package. You can learn a great deal about different franchises including addresses, whom to contact, number of locations, and capital investment required, by referring to the *Franchise Opportunity Handbook* published by the Department of Commerce, Washington, D.C. 20402. Also consult Dunn and Bradstreet and the Better Business Bureau to find out the financial standing and business reputation of the franchisor. (See the section at the back of this chapter for other recommended reading.)

THE LEGAL ASPECTS

The peculiarities of your business and your present financial position will determine which form of ownership will best suit your needs.

- Sole proprietorship
- Partnership, general or limited
- Corporation or subchapter S corporation

The difference between these structures is what will affect your personal liability and your tax position.

Sole Proprietorship

This is the simplest and least expensive way to start a business. As sole proprietor, the profits belong to you and you have total authority over the business. You may need to file for a business license or tax number issued by the Department of Consumer Affairs. Check with your local Chamber of Commerce to see if this applies in your area. In any case, they can advise you of any restrictions that may apply. There are usually no special legal restrictions when you set up a sole proprietorship.

As sole proprietor, *you* assume all liabilities and debts of the business. Your income directly reflects the revenue or losses of the business. You will need to protect your income with disability insurance and you will need to protect your already acquired assets with liability insurance.

Partnerships

Partnerships are similar to sole proprietorships in that the individuals are liable and taxed at the personal income level. Partners are all individually liable for the firm's obligations to the same unlimited degree. Partnerships are easier and less expensive than corporations to set up but more complicated than sole proprietorships. Here two or more fast-trackers are combining interests, ideas, and wealth for the profit. Perhaps the most vulnerable area of a partnership is choosing the right partner. From our research we learned it is fairly easy to set up a partnership, but hard and often unpleasant to break up. Always draw up a partnership agreement to protect your interests and the interests of the business. It is necessary to consult with an attorney and an accountant for this purpose.

General Partner

The general partner usually reaps the greatest rewards. Because the financial rewards are greater (as a general partner), you assume the financial and liability obligation. Also, each partner is a principle; you share:

1. The hands-on-burden of decision making.
2. The right to an equal share of the profits and the losses.
3. Upon liquidation and after all creditors are paid, each partner may receive in cash his/her share of the partnership's assets.

Limited Partner

A limited partner risks only his agreed upon investment in the business. A limited partner does not take an active role in the management of the corporation.

A Corporation

This type of business costs the most money to set up. There are government restrictions and regulations that vary from state to state that must be followed. Under the corporate umbrella you are protected against personal liability, unless you sign away that right (i.e., if you personally sign for and guarantee a loan to the corporation, you are liable should the business default). Please note that a personal service corporation does not limit your personal liability. Check with your accountant for further information. Corporations are formed for profit, and ownership is represented by shares of stock. A board of directors, elected by the shareholders, dictates policy and conducts business on a day-to-day basis. Capital is easiest to raise by selling stock or shares in your business. Do be aware of double taxation. This is a real factor of corporate life. The corporation pays a corporate tax, based on its income, and the owner pays a tax on his/her income from the corporation as well.

Subchapter S Corporation

A corporation with a maximum of 10 shareholders in which the profit of the corporation is not subject to corporate taxation rates is called a subchapter S corporation. Each shareholder reports his or her share of the corporate income and any dividends received on the individual tax return, offsetting income from other sources. In all other respects, an S corporation is treated as any other corporate entity.

If all of this has your head spinning, relax! To get the most accurate, up-to-date, and informed advice on how to set up your business, you absolutely must speak with:

- Your banker
- Your accountant
- Your attorney
- Your insurance agent

If possible, speak also with other fast-trackers who have succeeded in a similar business. Listen and learn from their experiences.

Keep in mind that most businesses fail due to poor management, *not* lack of funds. Educate yourself about good business management. Your local college may offer courses on entrepreneurships and management techniques. Your school or local library is a terrific source for how-to material and miscellaneous information.

INDUSTRY HOT SPOTS FOR ENTREPRENEURS —

Service businesses are experiencing continued growth and will continue to generate more income as millions of baby boomers head toward their middle years (35–50). Particularly high growth areas are:

- Financial services
- Fast foods
- Insurance
- Physical fitness
- Legal services
- Mail order
- Information systems, computers
- Geriatric care
- Hazardous waste management
- Drug rehabilitation

Women are the rising stars of entrepreneurship. They are opening small businesses at more than twice the rate of men. Women-owned businesses are the fastest growing segment of the small business community. Few women ventured into entrepreneurial pursuits in the 1950s, 1960s, and 1970s. Often those that did started a bakery or boutique or decorating firm, all low-overhead ventures that were extensions of the homemaking role. We cheer them for their courage and because they were pioneers of their time. The woman entrepreneur of today is likely to start her company with the help of professional contacts, financial savvy, a sophisticated business plan, and a heightened desire to make money in order to maintain and improve her lifestyle.

Most of the fast-track women we interviewed were:

- Well-educated (though some were not)
- All had a "sixth" sense for business
- Most had worked in their fields before starting their own business

- All liked making money
- All were excited by business possibilities

Overall, they agreed, and we do too, that the entrepreneur spirit must be in your blood. Okay, you've identified yourself as a budding entrepreneur—you're ambitious, enthusiastic, and you want to make it on your own. You even have an idea for a million dollar business, now what? The next step is to *finance* your idea.

GAINING FINANCIAL BACKING

There are two ways you can go about raising the cash you need:

- You can borrow the money
- You can take a partner, in one form or another

If you borrow the money, you have obtained debt capital and you have obligated yourself to pay interest to the lender. You do not, under the usual circumstances, give the lender ownership or control.

If you take a partner, you have obtained equity capital and you have obligated yourself to pay a portion of your future profits to the investor, based on an agreed-upon percentage. Further, the investor has bought the privilege of having some say in the control of the business, also based on an agreed upon percentage.

Now make a list of all possible investors. The most obvious, of course, are family members, friends, and business associates. Share your idea, perhaps offer something in return—a portion of the profit, a "piece of the action." Consider outside investors or friends of friends who may have extra cash and are willing to take a risk.

Bank financing is a strong possibility. A personal loan may be enough to get you started, particularly if there is no inventory involved, as in a service business. If a larger loan is needed, the bank may require you to submit a proposal. They may ask for a co-signer or collateral, such as real estate, stocks and bonds, or a savings passbook. It is good business to get to know the loan officer at your local bank. Use him or her as a source of financial advice or as a sounding board for new ways to pursue profits.

What Is Venture Capital?

A person who invests in a small business enterprise is called a venture capitalist. Venture capitalists are high-risk money lenders (sophisticated investors). They are willing to take a *greater risk*, expecting a *greater return* on their money. For taking the risks, the venture capitalist may get a percentage of the equity. He or she may also expect to participate in managing the company. The venture capitalist may want to be able to convert his or her interest into cash at a future date. Be sure to protect yourself.

If you are looking for a lot of money to start up your new business, you might consider this money-raising alternative. Ask your lawyer or accountant or investment banker for referrals.

OPM (Other People's Money)

OPM is a simple postulate of free enterprise. The clearest example of using "other people's money" we know is credit. You buy goods on credit. The terms call for (demand) payment in 30, 60, or 90 days from the time of delivery. Suppliers and wholesalers are liberal in extending credit; after all, they want your business. If your business requires an inventory, OPM could be the tool for you. Also, consider barter or stock for services. Build up a credit line with your bank and borrow.

Raise cash by selling stock. If you incorporate your business, you can raise capital (often large sums) by issuing stock. This is called equity financing. The stockholders actually own the corporation. With stock ownership comes the right to:

- Participate in corporate earnings
- Receive the assets upon liquidation
- Vote to elect a board of directors

As a shareholder your liability is limited to the value of or the number of shares of stock you own.

WORDS OF CAUTION

This chapter would be incomplete without a word of caution. The Small Business Administration advises us that 50 percent of all new businesses fail within 36 months. The dangers are:

- Undercapitalization
- Lack of know-how
- Beginning an impossible task
- Cash flow (not enough money to carry on until payment starts coming in)
- Failure to develop an adequate or realistic long-range business plan
- Short-term lease (this can put you out of business or choke you)

Some Do's and Don'ts

- Do be prudent and conservative to avoid underestimating your start-up costs. Also, avoid overestimating your profits.

- Do consider whether there is sufficient demand for your product or service.
- Do select a business you understand and invest only what you are willing to lose.
- Don't rely on anyone else to supervise production, personnel, or cash.
- Don't over-extend yourself.
- Don't grow too fast.
- Don't live it up too early.

Drifting from one day to the next guarantees failure sooner or later. On the other hand, even a one-year plan provides objectives and direction and an ultimate goal. Write your plan down. Plan for the future.

Sometimes entrepreneurs fail due to poor judgment and ill-informed decision making. Use your good sense and draw upon outside resources as necessary to help make sound business decisions. Don't try to go it alone. Build a network of support within the framework of your business and at home.

Understanding the finances of your business should be considered a top priority. Avoid taking on more debt than the company can handle. Retain as much capital as possible. Keep costs down. Plan an austerity program for a least the first couple of years. Very few start-up entrepreneurs can afford flashy cars or large salaries (at least initially). Keep looking at the figures—they tell the story. Remember good planning is good business.

EARNING POWER

It was virtually impossible to document entrepreneurial earning power. We did note the lifestyles of the successful fast-trackers we spoke with and we have every indication they were earning in excess of $50,000 yearly (and many double or triple this amount). One successful woman summed it up this way, "Earning enough money to support myself is a source of great power and pleasure."

LAST MINUTE TIPS . . .

- Check with your local college. Most colleges offer course-work in entrepreneurship, over 250 offer entrepreneurial curriculums.
- Attend seminars, often given by successful fast-trackers.
- Visit your local library.
- Check Business Periodical Index & Wall Street Journal Index for a wealth of magazine articles (too numerous to mention here).
- Ask a librarian to direct you to the "Vertical File." Here you will find a collection of pamphlets directed at improving your chances for success.

Trade publications and associations could aid you with technical knowledge. Ask questions and speak with successful fast-trackers. Call the local Chamber of Commerce.

GLOSSARY

Capital:
Net worth of the individual or business; combination of fixed and liquid assets after the deduction of liabilities; also the funds used to start up or capitalize a business.

Corporation:
A group of people who get a charter granting them legal powers, rights, privileges, and liabilities distinct from those of individuals in the group. A corporation can buy, sell and inherit property.

Debt Capital:
Borrowed money that must be repaid with interest but which, normally, does not give the lender any ownership control.

Entrepreneur:
One who organizes and directs a business undertaking, assuming the risk for the sake of profits.

Equity Capital:
Ownership dollars that are not repaid but instead entitle the investor to a say in a business and a percentage of future profits.

Franchisee:
The individual who invests in an enterprise and operates it.

Franchisor:
The company or partner who is selling the image, product and expertise.

Investor:
One who puts money into businesses, real estate, stocks or bonds for the purpose of obtaining an income or profit.

Liability:
Legal obligation to make good any loss or damage that occurs in a transaction; responsibility.

Partnership:
An association of two or more people who contribute money or property to carry on a joint business and who share profits or losses in agreed upon proportion.

Personal Service Corporation (PC):
Usually a legal set-up to protect doctors, lawyers or other professionals. A financial arrangement.

Sole Proprietor:
A legal form of business in which one person supplies all the capital needs of the business; therefore, the company is owned by one person.

Stock:
Shares of corporate capital, or the certificates of ownership representing them.

Strategy:
A plan

Undercapitalization:
The situation existing when a firm doesn't have any cash to cover operating expenses.

Venture Capitalists:
Investors who make available capital dollars for a variety of enterprises, expecting a significant return on their investment.

WHAT YOU SHOULD BE READING

Changing Times
220 East 42nd Street
New York, NY 10017
212-599-0454

Entrepreneur
645 Fifth Avenue
New York, NY 10022
212-303-2711

Inc.
342 Madison Avenue
New York, NY 10173
212-986-2161

Money
Time, Inc.
Time & Life Building
Rockefeller Center
New York, NY 10020
212-522-1212

Venture
521 Fifth Avenue
New York, NY 10175
212-682-7373

ORGANIZATIONS FOR MORE INFORMATION

American Women's Economic Development Corporation
1270 Avenue of Americas
New York, NY 10020

Center for Entrepreneurial Management
29 Greene Street
New York, NY 10013

Federal Trade Commission
Washington, DC 20580

National Association of Women Business Owners
2000 P Street NW
Washington, DC 20036

National Federation of Independent Business
150 West 20 Avenue
San Mateo, CA 94403

Small Business Administration
1441 L Street NW
Washington, DC 20416

Small Business Council
Chamber of Commerce
(Contact local office, see your phone directory.)

A FINAL WORD

We would like to reiterate that we clearly believe a fast-tracking career *is* worth pursuing. It offers frequent emotional highs, easy access to material goods and, in general, a very comfortable way of living. However, in all fairness to our readers we want to remind you that fast-tracking also means pressure, frequent personal sacrifices and, in some cases, the inability ever to be satisfied with what you have.

Our culture equates fast-tracking with success and, as an article in *Newsday* recently stated, "Success. The drug of the 80's. More fashionable even than cocaine, and probably just as addictive. It's the high for our times. Everybody seems to want it, and nobody ever seems to have enough." We feel that last sentence is the key. Being a fast-tracker can and does generate enormous personal satisfaction for those who make it, but we sincerely believe that once there, you need to step back and evaluate what you have and what you want. As all of the fast-trackers we interviewed told us, you need to be willing to give something up to get the fast-track career you desire. During one of our interviews, our subject noted, "I keep asking myself what are my priorities. Up until now, making money has been the main focus of my life. Intellectually, I feel I can't make money that important, but I'm in a field and position now where if I don't pursue something so lucrative as this, I feel like I'll be copping out. I do know that one of these days, I think I'll say enough is enough."

We've outlined for you areas where we think there is tremendous potential in fast-track success. Your path is not by any means limited to these fields. We urge you to explore an area which interests you and which will offer you the kind of physical and emotional lifestyle you want. Fast-tracking can be exciting and fun, but it's not worth doing if you don't enjoy the career you're involved in.

Good Luck!

INDEX